WHAT PEOPLE ARE SAYING ABOUT

PLAY FROM YOUR FUCKING HEART

Jerry Hyde is the magpie of wisdom, delivering it in the way all great tricksters do, ass backwards.

If you are like me and self-help books make you cringe and yet there is a nagging feeling that you're a bit bored shitless of how you see the world, Jerry is like the crazy man you meet randomly in the pub that makes magical fucked-up sense.

I read this book while travelling to work. Suddenly commuting became a rock and roll journey towards myself. Don't be a pussy – read it.
Sam Roddick, founder of Coco de Mer and pleasure activist

As a self-confessed 'artist/rocker' who likes to live life on the wild-side but then ends up reaching for some self-improvement guide to redeem myself of guilt, this book actually says fuck it... live the life you want to! This is a dangerously insightful and brutally frank glimpse at life through the eyes of Jerry Hyde... Moral depravity and genius clash head on and hand in hand... couldn't put the fucker down.
Darryl Gates, Diamond Jacks Tattoo, London

Wake up and celebrate – Jerry Hy
Jonny Phillips, actor and director

I've had the privilege of working w.... jerry for ten years – if our relationship started as a conventional therapist/client scenario it soon became apparent it wasn't like what I'd seen in the films. If the initial topic was about being an alcoholic/victim/loser it soon became about so much more. Our work together took me on a journey within. It wasn't like he was offering me the answers, more he was prompting me to ask the questions. I remember him telling me that a client had left him because he didn't feel like he was being offered enough advice. Makes you think if there was someone out there with all the answers they'd write a book & everyone in the world would buy it & we'd all be ok ... wouldn't we? So instead READ THIS. Less of a Self Help book more a Help Yourself book. A book where the learnings & quotes of Bill Hicks mean as much as those of Carl Jung. Where a viewing of Apocalypse Now will give you more insight than the collective readings of any organised religion. This book will instill bravery in yourself, your fuck ups will start to have a meaning beyond *"I can't believe I fucked up again"*, they will be the source of your wisdom. This book says don't trust anyone who say's they've got the answer to your problems, just trust yourself.

But be warned, the cult begins here.

Sean Rowley, Guilty Pleasures

Reading Jerry Hyde's latest book is like having a transcendental late-night chat with the cool big brother you wish you'd had. Unapologetically honest, rebellious and thought-provoking, Jerry's direct conversational style grabs you hard by the ear from the first page, and keeps yanking until you're paying attention and sitting right next him on the 'ledge beyond the ledge'. With your legs dangling precariously over the abyss, you peer down at the mundane life you once led and wonder what the fuck you were doing before you read this book. Jerry Hyde pulls no punches, in fact he's got a mean left hook, but instead of 'knocking your lights out' he turns them on.

Melissa Unger, Creative Consultant & Founder of Seymour Projects

Jerry's book will ruin your life. And you'll thank him for it.

John Williams, author of *Screw Work Let's Play*

Like many others I first met Jerry Hyde after he was recommended to me as a therapist. Within 30 seconds of meeting him I decided I didn't like him and wasn't going to tell him anything personal at all. After 30 minutes I had told him things I hadn't even told myself! That was in 1998 and I went on to spend the next ten years participating in the first of several ongoing men's therapy groups that he setup. There were a few constants throughout this time: an exciting, slightly dangerous tension between suspicion and commitment from the members; an increasing understanding that the group thrives on the creative freedom of the individual; and Jerry's unfailing professionalism, kindness and care.

Jerry has developed a therapeutic style that is truly his own and this book is a provocative, funny and revealing presentation of his ideas. Its rock 'n roll flippancy belies the wisdom amassed from 20 years of experience and while I might retain some suspicion of the language (I don't know whether to hide it from my kids or not), I felt deeply moved when I completed it. I don't think Jerry has the slightest desire to be a guru: his work inhabits an almost contradictory world where those who are really inspired by him feel no need to be like him! Enlightenment indeed.

Dominic Murcott, composer and educator

I don't know anything about Therapy and only slightly more about Rock 'n Roll, but what I do know is that most people in the modern world are definitely not Awake. Sedated by our culture and hiding beneath veils of assumed personality, we are Souls in hiding.

Who can say what it takes to Wake Up? How to be fully conscious in this crazy pulsating mystery that is Life? There is a fine art to surfing the paradox of losing the self and Finding the Self. The way is not what our sleepyheads think it is.

If you really must read another book before surfacing from

your slumbers then read this one! Don't be lulled into thinking that this is just another innocent meandering yarn in the comfy web of your dream, the rude crowing rooster resounds throughout. Refreshingly free from New Age twaddle, uncompromisingly honest and with some genuinely helpful tips, this may be the literary equivalent of a zen alarm clock.
Claire Heron, Enlightenment Intensive Master

Hi Jerry, you may NOT use the title, *The Keith Richards Health Plan.*
Fran Curtis, Executive Vice President, Rogers & Cowan, PR and Marketing for The Rolling Stones

Play From Your Fucking Heart

A somewhat twisted escape plan for people who usually hate self-help books

Play From Your Fucking Heart

A somewhat twisted escape plan for people who usually hate self-help books

Jerry Hyde

Winchester, UK
Washington, USA

First published by Soul Rocks Books, 2014
Soul Rocks Books is an imprint of John Hunt Publishing Ltd., Laurel House, Station Approach,
Alresford, Hants, SO24 9JH, UK
office1@jhpbooks.net
www.johnhuntpublishing.com
www.soulrocks-books.com

For distributor details and how to order please visit the 'Ordering' section on our website.

Text copyright: Jerry Hyde 2013

ISBN: 978 1 78279 408 0

A CIP catalogue record for this book is available from the British Library.

Design: Lee Nash
Cover design: Robert Crumb

Printed and bound by CPI Group (UK) Ltd, Croydon, CR0 4YY

We operate a distinctive and ethical publishing philosophy in all
areas of our business, from our global network of authors to
production and worldwide distribution.

CONTENTS

Introduction by Shivam O'Brien   1

Chapter 1: The Way of Gonzo   3

Chapter 2: Hit Your Thumb Repeatedly with a 20 oz Estwing Surestrike All Steel Straight Claw Hammer...   21

Chapter 3: How to Polish a Turd...   39

Chapter 4: Play from Your Fucking Heart...   49

Chapter 5: Think Like a Serial Killer...   66

Chapter 6: Own Your Inner Keef   77

Chapter 7: Pablo Picasso was Never Called an Asshole   87

Chapter 8: I'd Love to Spill the Beans with You All Night   99

Chapter 9: This Thing's Bigger Than the Both of Me   115

Chapter 10: The Brown Acid Isn't Specifically Too Good...   126

Chapter 11: The Secret of Success   135

Chapter 12: Eat. Shit. Die.   136

Suggested Further Reading and Other Great Shit   152

Big Ups   155

For Noor and Tara

This is the rock 'n' roll life, and you had to invent it as you went along. There was no textbook to say how you operate this machinery.
Keith Richards

If you're going to try, go all the way. Otherwise, don't even start. This could mean losing girlfriends, wives, relatives and maybe even your mind. It could mean not eating for three or four days. It could mean freezing on a park bench. It could mean jail. It could mean derision. It could mean mockery – isolation. Isolation is the gift. All the others are a test of your endurance, of how much you really want to do it. And, you'll do it, despite rejection and the worst odds. And it will be better than anything else you can imagine. If you're going to try, go all the way. There is no other feeling like that. You will be alone with the gods, and the nights will flame with fire. You will ride life straight to perfect laughter. It's the only good fight there is.
Charles Bukowski

Keith went over the edge years ago. He went over the fuckin' edge and everyone thought that's it right, that's Keith gone, and then they looked over the edge and there's a fuckin' ledge and he had landed on it. There's a ledge... beyond the edge.
Bill Hicks

Any spiritual teacher worth their salt has already pressed the self-destruct button.
Claire Heron, Enlightenment Intensive Master

Introduction by Shivam O'Brien

I met Jerry through an email. He sent me a few video samples that were to illustrate his approach to his work, including (a refreshing wild card for a London therapist who might have some sort of reputation to uphold) a definition of enlightenment from a very hard-hitting American standup icon. There was nothing in Jerry's email to suggest he was a reliable, well-sorted, fully certified, emotionally flat, socially predictable therapist.

I liked him straight away.

And vision quest, no less, was part of the therapy! Impressed that this guy had seemingly retained some natural, trustworthy wildness, I invited him to my fire... that's a Celtic roundhouse, that used to be a tipi, that became a community in a wild valley in Wales where we all... well Jerry'll mention that later.

Only when I met twenty-five of his 'clients', a couple of years later, did I realise just how much this honest, straight talking, ex-rock and roller therapist meant to so many people. Without voicing one politically or therapeutically correct sentence, without playing any leadership tactic or trip, without throwing out any ideas that might have pulled a 'wow,' he commanded utter respect and trust from some pretty world-hardened musicians, edge of the envelope creative types and even a fair proportion of sane friendly professional Londoners.

These people trusted him pretty much for the same reasons I did. He wasn't ever going to say anything big about who he was, where he'd been or what he knew. Yet he held – without being overly visible. He commanded – without any orders. He nurtured – without intruding.

Jerry doesn't hold out any 'fits all' answers, or policy, or correctness, however, he is humbly real and doesn't ever give away that behind the dry humour and fain Englishness there is a sharply astute, highly principled adult male, devoted to truth and gentleness and one that can't be bought at any price.

That's why I like him. That's why I am writing this introduction. And that's why you should read *Play From Your Fucking Heart* – apart from the fact that he's a highly entertaining writer.

This book is like sitting in Jerry's wonderful London pad having a long growling and grinning chat about life, living and learning. He won't be trying to sell you anything, it's a real sharing of loves, failures, insights and joys that you can put in your shoes and walk forward with.

Jerry, as usual, is saying what he wants to say in a language anyone can understand and you won't have to join in with any pseudo-psycho talk or have your intellect bombarded with smart ideas. The smart ideas are there alright, plenty of 'em, but it's one human to another, speaking easy, heart to heart.

Read on, if you're in search of satisfaction, Jerry Hyde is plucking some real and raw notes here – a Rolling Stone in the Delta of Healing.

Shivam O'Brien, Galway, Oct 20th, 2013

Chapter 1

The Way of Gonzo

Be daring, be different, be impractical, be anything that will assert integrity of purpose and imaginative vision against the play-it-safers, the creatures of the commonplace, the slaves of the ordinary.
Cecil Beaton said that. Fuck yeah!

Most people go through life dreading they'll have a traumatic experience. Freaks were born with their trauma. They've already passed their test in life. They're aristocrats.
Diane Arbus said that...

Hunter and I never got proper journalistic accreditation to go anywhere. Nobody was giving us passes to go in here or there. We always had to somehow talk our way in.
Ralph Steadman said that...

Look, you've got it all wrong! You don't need to follow me! You don't need to follow anybody! You've got to think for yourselves! You're all individuals!
Brian of Nazareth said that...

Beginning a book is like beginning a relationship – you start out full of hope, excitement and expectation, checking out the exterior, the cover, then maybe spending a bit of time flicking through a few pages, testing the water, looking for signs that it has substance and intrigue until slowly you get drawn in and...

Actually, y'know what? Fuck it – stop that train of thought, I'm boring myself already, I'm not kicking this off with an analogy, it's *way* too early to go all Forrest Gump on you – there'll be plenty of time for that later...

The real point is – why should you read beyond the first page?

And perhaps more importantly, why should you trust *me*?

The simple answer to that is – *you shouldn't*. You shouldn't trust *me* at all (actually it's a pretty good rule not to trust *anyone* who uses the word should or shouldn't).

That's what that book *If you meet the Buddha on the Road Kill Him* was all about – if he *says* he's the Buddha then he's *not* the Buddha 'cos *you* are the Buddha. Not that I've read it, it's just one of those great books that you don't have to read 'cos it's all in the title, like *Feel the Fear and do it Anyway*; pick it up, look at the cover, put it back on the shelf, job done.

I'd love to write a book like that.

The original working title of this book was *The Keith Richards Health Plan*, but Keith's people thought that it probably wasn't such a fantastic idea after all and his lawyers are bigger than my lawyers. In fact, I don't *have* lawyers. I don't even have *people*. But even that title, much as I loved it, didn't quite have that 'does what it says on the can' immediacy.

I'd tweak the Buddha book title a little, something like *'If You Meet the Buddha on the Road Mug Him'* because:

(a) I'm against capital punishment and if we kill everyone who goes around claiming to be a messiah there'd be a lot of dead sports presenters lying around.

(b) It's a bit of a baby bathwater scenario, a lot of gurus, spiritual teachers and even therapists have some clever things to say, and they're worth mugging for their wisdom.

One person worth mugging is my friend John Williams, author of the great *Screw Work Let's Play*, who taught me this easy little process by which you can find your life's purpose, your own unique message to the world.

He said – imagine that you have the opportunity to meet yourself as a small child, with all that you know now as an adult. What message would you would want to give to the mini you?

Try it – it's a killer exercise and might really help

This is what came to me – quick as a flash.

"Don't trust *anyone* who tells you that they know what's right for you. Trust *yourself* – YOU are the expert."

And that goes for you too. Trust yourself – you bought, borrowed or stole this book right? Something in YOU *knew...* You're the expert, of you, no one else. And anyone who says they're an expert of anything, let alone you, is to be treated with great suspicion. Expertise is cool, but experts have stopped learning.

My maternal Grandparents, Pete and Alice Muckley, had a big hand in drumming that one into me. *"Don't trust authority,"* Pete used to warn me. *"Look what happened on the Somme."*

You just can't argue with stats like that.

And as the not quite as impressive as my Grandfather but nevertheless brilliant controversial Rolls Royce collecting possibly assassinated by the CIA charismatic unblinking contra-dictory trickster and sex guru Bhagwan Shree Rajneesh, or Osho as he was perhaps better known, put it in the very first of his Ten Commandments:

"Never obey anyone's command unless it is coming from within you also."

Or more simply in the words of Bob Dylan, *"don't follow leaders, watch the parkin' meters"*. Then again you've got Shakespeare who must have been abducted by aliens for the amount of shit that he *really* understood; I mean, *"to thine own self be true,"* how good is that? And then you've got the great beast himself, the much maligned bad boy of magic, Aleister Crowley with, *"do what thou wilt shall be the whole of the Law..."*

Oh, and Osho's third Commandment's pretty cool too:

"Truth is within you, do not search for it elsewhere."

Which kind of makes this book redundant.

The End

Oh – you're still there...

Sorry, I was distracted listening to this really rather *far out* Indian slide guitar player called Debashish Bhattacharya – think Ry Cooder on acid – but given that I haven't lost you, *all we are saaaaaaaying* is that this book will offer you absolutely *NO NEW WISDOM WHATSOEVER.*

Because (drumroll)

You already know it all.

Honest. Trust me. NO! Don't trust me, trust yourself – oh fuck it...

And so, anyway, what *is* the promise of *Play From Your Fucking Heart*? What's it selling – it must be selling something right? If it's not new wisdom or happiness, what exactly are you gonna *get* from investing your precious time in reading this book?

A glimmer. A glimmer that there is something more, perhaps much, much more, to life than you realised. Maybe a flashback, a fleeting memory of a time in your life when you *knew* that anything was possible, a time before you became cautious and wary. As a culture we have never been more sedated by technology and gadgets and comforting distractions from life – to *Play From Your Fucking Heart* is to wake up, to go all the way, to be alone with the gods, to live **LIFE** in perfect **laughter** free from fear that anaesthetises and deadens, to press the self-destruct button on mundanity and break the chains of the slaves of the ordinary.

In *The Top Five Regrets of the Dying: A Life Transformed by the Dearly Departing* palliative nurse Bronnie Ware, who counselled the dying in their last days, revealed the most common regret:

"I wish I'd had the courage to live a life true to myself, not the life others expected of me."

Play From Your Fucking Heart...

Is the antidote.

And in a way you could call this an eco book, as its entire contents have been recycled. Y'see I'm writing with the stated belief that there *is* NO new wisdom, that in fact the experience that *you* the reader has whenever you read something and go, *'oh wow, that is deep'* – is one of already *knowing*, of a part of yourself that was already there waking up to an eternal collective truth, and that the writer acts as a trigger or stimulant rather than as a wise sage or guru or clever bastard who 'knows all'.

One clever bastard wise sage guru mad Irish builder stroke shaman I trust – and there are *very* few that I do – is Shivam O'Brien, introducer of this book and tribal leader at the mighty Spirit Horse Community in Wales, and, more to the point, Gonzo as *fuck* (more of him later).

Shivam was not only responsible for turning me onto Debashish Bhattacharya but also Sri Nisargadatta Maharaj and his book *I Am That*. Now there's a humble and profound tome, and it illustrates my point perfectly because in 1973, forty years before this book, he wrote,

> *did I ever tell you that you do not know and, therefore, you are inferior? Let those who invented such distinctions prove them. I do not claim to know what you do not. In fact, I know much less than you do.*

And I really do know much less than you; about you, and many other things.

And what's more, the older I get the more I realise how little I know, the wiser I get the more I see my own ignorance. It's vast...

Of course many 'self-help' books are written by self-appointed gurus – some good, some not – and whilst I have at times benefited greatly from these writings, each time I read something and go – oh wow, that's *really clever shit* – I then almost immediately read something else and go – hold on you *fucker*, that stuff I just read that seemed so fresh and exciting and *new* was just a rehash of what the Vedics/NativeAmericans/Sufis/Aborigines/Pagans/Tibetans/Druids/Buddhists and/or Mayans were saying five/ten/fifteen/twenty thousand years ago...

That in itself is not a criticism but an acknowledgement that the writers that have most impressed me – Osho, George Gurdjieff, Eckhart Tolle, David Deida, Deepak Chopra to name a few – are really just great translators, they have all taken ancient teachings and revamped and repackaged them for a contemporary audience.

And so this is what I'm offering – a collection of all my experiences and learning from over twenty years of psychotherapy practice and participation (with doses of tantra, paganism, shamanism and psychedelic exploration thrown in) presented, I hope, in a fresh and accessible way, avoiding 'therapy speak' with the aim being to communicate valuable concepts without intimidating or excluding you, 'cos all too often I've read important works that have left me excited but overwhelmed, with a sense of how unattainable the teachings appear to be.

Therapy is no longer taboo – it's a multi-million pound mainstream industry and people are hungry for change. With *Play From Your Fucking Heart* I'm attempting to offer a fresh and irreverent perspective to some of the fundamentals of self-help and personal development, taking therapy down to street level, a rock and roll guidebook to the science of the bleedin' obvious.

I chose to write this book partly in response to people asking *'when are you going to write a book?'* To be honest, I couldn't see the point in a market that seemed flooded with self-help books but then it came to me – I *know* the creative world, not only do I know it but I've *failed* in just about every area from music, theatre, film and writing, I've lived the life, taken the drugs, experienced the highs and lows, survived and come out (more or less) intact.

Then, more importantly, the title came to me and I realised that there is a gap in the market for a more 'twisted' self-help book, a book for people who wouldn't normally be seen *dead* reading a self-help book – fucked up rock'n rollers, scooter riding creatives, left-field crazies, dope fiends, Hoxton untouchables, underground eccentrics, midlife burn-outs and hipsters trapped in mainstream suits and lives wanting an *escape plan*.

Those of you who, dare I say, it, live on the ledge

… beyond the edge.

My kinda people.

Outsiders.

Now hold your wild horses – don't feel downhearted…

Look at it like this – in days gone by, the second worst penalty after the death sentence was exile. That's gotta tell you something about just how much we all fear exclusion from the tribe no matter how many times you ask Marlon what's he's rebelling against and he replies *"whaddaya-got?"*

But I bring good news people – way, *way* out there, far from the safety of the tribe, deep in the wasteland on the ledge beyond the edge, there is a tribe, *another* tribe, a tribe of exiles, a tribe of misfits, a tribe of *outsiders* who await you with open arms saying *'come brother, come sister, we have a place for you by the fire and food aplenty and dry clothes and shelter'* and you fall to your knees and give thanks crying *'Lawsy Lawsy, good Lord willin' an' the creek don't rise, I HAVE come home'* or some such authentic Frontier gibberish – I'll leave that to you to fill in the gaps.

But you get my point right?

You're not alone.

I get a kick out of being an outsider constantly. It allows me to be creative. I don't like anything in the mainstream and they don't like me.

Bill Hicks said that…

I should probably interject at this point and, just in case the title of this book wasn't enough to give it away, point out that I'm a massive Stones freak. I don't mean I'm one of those people who sold the house and the kids in order to follow them around the world on tour, but as an entity they had a huge impact on forming my life. The Stones were somehow, inexplicably, my introduction to the esoteric, to the mystic, to the shadow side, to the forbidden, to the exotic, to the unknowable. Whilst The Beatles woke me up and turned me onto music in the first place, The Stones drew my attention to something that I still find hard to put into words, to something sensual and dark and pleasurable and very much alive. When I listened to The Beatles I was intrigued by the complexity and wonder of their accomplished musicianship, when I put a Stones album on I could *smell* them.

The Stones provided a soundtrack for my entire life.

They changed the way I looked at the world.

They made me feel that I *belonged*.

I'm dyslexic. That was my ticket to the outer edges. I was one of the early Ritalin kids. I remember when the IQ test results came back from the child psychologist as being in the mid 140s, my Dad's puzzled response was, *"well – if you're not stupid... you must be lazy."*

The shrink in charge of the fiasco that was my school experience said, *"we normally give these pills to fat ladies, but we're going to try them on you,"* and so for the next three years, breakfast became a twenty milligram tablet of methylphenidate marked Ciba on the side. Wikipedia states that the drug:

> *possesses some structural and pharmacological similarities to cocaine, though it is less potent and longer in duration. Psychotic symptoms from long term methylphenidate use can include hearing voices, visual hallucinations, urges to harm oneself, severe anxiety, euphoria, grandiosity, paranoid delusions, confusion, increased aggression and irritability.*

What could possibly go wrong?

So learning has always been a struggle, and as a practitioner I have always striven to make things as simplistic as possible, to make what appears complex immediate and accessible and I've always rejected the idea of the therapist as the clever, all-knowing, enlightened one. My approach in my daily work is to make sure I'm firmly *off* the pedestal and these attitudes have strongly influenced and shaped this book. Psychotherapeutic concepts can be intimidating, but strip away the loftiness and you discover that it's actually very simple, which is what I mean by the science of the bleedin' obvious.

When people ask me what I do I always hesitate – I hate that question; it makes me almost as uncomfortable as going through customs. In my twenties I was a drug crazed rock'n roll guitar player in a group called The Batniks – a band once described as *'so underground that no one knows they're there...'* I moonlighted as a stagehand in film, TV and theatre when not signing on, living a colourful and impoverished life as an East End squatter and self-intentioned drop-out – not that I ever dropped in long enough to drop out...

In my thirties I cleaned up my act and worked as a psychotherapist for 13 years; I then tried calling myself a coach – why not? Everyone else does. I've been to India and trained in tantra but that doesn't quite qualify me to call myself a Guru, and I've been buried alive and fasted in the wilderness for days on end but that doesn't quite make me a Shaman... and Psycho-therapeutic Shamanic Coaching Guru is a real mouthful.

Over the years people started calling me a Gonzo Therapist, and I guess that'll do – I'm stuck with it now anyway – but when it comes to marketing it's not really a winner because NO ONE KNOWS WHAT IT *MEANS*...

So, before I lay any of my twisted ideas on you, I better clear that one up.

Gonzo therapist?

Gonzo therapist...

Ok, now... that very well may mean absolutely *nothing* to you, but – given that the universe has placed this book in your hands, chances are that YOU my friend...

Are a Gonzo seeker.

Which rumour has it may well in fact be the name of the very tribe that lives way out on the ledge beyond the edge (bank details and cult indoctrination specifics will follow later in this chapter.)

So what... *is*... Gonzo?

Let's start with Wikipedia:

The word Gonzo was first used in 1970 to describe an article by Hunter S. Thompson, who later popularized the style. The term has since been applied to other subjective artistic endeavours. Gonzo journalism is a style of journalism that is written subjectively, often including the reporter as part of the story via a first-person narrative.

Gonzo journalism disregards the 'polished' edited product favoured by newspaper media and strives for a more gritty approach. Use of quotations, sarcasm, humour, exaggeration, and profanity is common.

Get the picture?

Then I started considering who my lifelong heroes were and that began to make sense of something, especially as I realised there was a commonality, a thread.

Apart from Keith Richards there was Hunter S. Thompson, Bill Hicks, John Lennon, Mick Jagger and Bob Dylan to name a few.

All, to my mind – Gonzo pioneers.

People who, you could argue – well I am anyway – in medieval times might well have had the role of The Fool.

So I began to look at the role of The Fool in historical culture.

And a quote from some obscure site struck me as pertinent:

The fool constantly questions our perceptions of wisdom and truth and their relationship to everyday experience. <u>The fool lifts the veil of authority, devoid of decorum, acting irreverently, unmasking the unpleasant aspects of power.</u>

Now, bear with me and remember that I'm trying to explain to you (and me – for we always write for ourselves) the qualities that make a Gonzo seeker.

This led me to Heyókȟa, and then things started to get *really* exciting.

The word Heyókȟa refers to the Lakota Indians' concept of a contrarian, jester, satirist or sacred clown.

(Keep Thompson, Hicks, Lennon and Jagger in mind as you read on).

Their satire presents important questions by fooling around. They ask difficult questions, and say things others are too afraid to say.

Principally, the Heyókȟa functions both as a mirror and a teacher, using extreme behaviours to mirror others, thereby forcing them to examine their own doubts, fears, hatreds, and weaknesses. Heyókȟas also have the power to heal emotional pain; such power comes from the experience of shame – they sing of shameful events in their lives, beg for food, and live as clowns. They provoke laughter in distressing situations of despair and provoke fear and chaos when people feel complacent and overly secure, to keep them from taking themselves too seriously or believing they are more powerful than they are.

In addition, sacred clowns serve an important role in shaping tribal codes. Heyókȟa's don't seem to care about taboos, rules, regulations, social norms, or boundaries. Paradoxically, however, it is by violating these norms and taboos that they help to define the accepted boundaries, rules, and societal guidelines for ethical and moral behaviour. This is because they are the only ones who can ask "Why?" about sensitive topics and employ satire to question the specialists and carriers of sacred knowledge or those in positions of power and authority. In doing so, they demonstrate concretely the theories of balance and imbalance. Their role is to penetrate deception, turn over rocks, and create a deeper awareness.

Now that to me… is *proper* Gonzo.

Knew a thing or two did those Lakotans.

Now I've been mostly going on, and on, and *on* about the importance of The Fool. But I also need to include another hero of mine, yet another Heyókȟa, George Ivanovich Gurdjieff.

George Ivanovich Gurdjieff (Armenian: Greek: Γεώργιος Γεωργιάδης, Russian: Гео́ргий Ива́нович Гюрджи́ев, January 13, 1866? – October 29, 1949) was a mystic and spiritual teacher. He called his discipline "The Work" (connoting "work on oneself") according to Gurdjieff's principles and instructions, or (originally) the "Fourth Way". Gurdjieff claimed that people cannot perceive reality in their current state because they do not possess consciousness but rather live in a state of a hypnotic "waking sleep".

"Man lives his life in sleep, and in sleep he dies." As a result of this condition each person perceives things from a completely subjective perspective. Gurdjieff stated that maleficent events such as wars and so on could not possibly take place if people were more awake. He asserted that people in their typical state function as unconscious automatons, but that one can "wake up" and become a different sort of human being altogether.

Did you get that bit?

Maleficent events such as wars and so on could not possibly take place if people were more awake.

Fuck…

Now, if you've made it this far, you'll probably have got your head around the connections I'm making between The Fool, Heyókȟa, and Gonzo. And if you took in the stuff about Heyókȟa then you will get the connection I'm making with Gurdjieff, Thompson, Hicks etc.

So – what defines a true Gonzo seeker?

A Gonzo seeker, whilst almost certainly being a habitual user of quotations, sarcasm, humour, exaggeration, and profanity, *realises* that one can 'wake up' and become a different sort of human being altogether.

A Gonzo seeker *questions* perceptions of wisdom and truth, lifts the veil of authority, acting irreverently, unmasking the unpleasant aspects of power, challenging the routine taken-for-granted aspects of daily rituals, asking difficult questions, and saying things others are too afraid to say.

A Gonzo seeker doesn't *care* about rules, regulations or social norms.

A Gonzo seeker would neither belong to any club that would have them as a member nor define themselves as a Gonzo seeker.

And above all the Gonzo seeker is *always* daring, different and impractical, asserting integrity of purpose and imaginative vision against the play-it-safers, the creatures of the common place, the slaves of the ordinary.

Welcome home.

Now, just before I wrap this chapter up there are a couple more points I need to make.

First off – and you may have got this already through your own keen powers of observation – I'm really quite fucked up. Sorry – but I am. And it's taken over twenty years of 'personal development' to get to this stage, and for that I make no apology.

Osho always said either be completely stupid, dumb, unaware and blind to anything other than your shitty existence, or go for the big one and full self-actualisation. It's the getting caught in the middle that *really* hurts.

And so I'm not saying I'm a car crash or that I'm (all that) dangerous, just that I inhabit that uncomfortable place in between ignorance and enlightenment.

The UKCP (that's the United Kingdom Council of Psychotherapists to you mere mortals) will probably have me whacked for revealing this but... do you know that most psychotherapists are deeply neurotic and fucked up? Like many psychiatrists are MAD? I don't know how it works with tantra and shamanism. Maybe all tantrikas have shit sex lives and shamans are afraid of dogs or summink.

I mentioned Shivam O'Brien earlier, and the reason I trust him is simple, it's because he wears his dysfunction on his sleeve, there's no bullshit and he's in a constant state of learning. That's the kind of qualification I'm looking for these days – I don't care too much for certificates. The real teachers tend to have *lived*.

I remember when it first dawned on me that my therapist wasn't exactly... *functioning* all that well. It really did my head in at first, but then after a while a kind of slow relief crept in – like therapists weren't part of some über master-race that I could never possibly be a member of. And in all honesty, if you're looking for a therapist it really pays to have one who's really been in the shit, otherwise how are they ever gonna know about life? From a text book? Remember what we said about Heyókȟas – they *'have the power to heal emotional pain; such power comes from the experience of shame.'*

Sometimes I feel over-qualified.

And sadly there's more and more battery-farmed therapists around than ever who read their Jung and Freud but never did an hour's work on *themselves* – I say get a fuckup any day, just make sure they're one step ahead and there are no blood stains on the couch.

But you see that's the magic, that's what I realised when I first saw a shrink when I was twenty-eight, it was like – *oh*, okay... so all the disasters in my life suddenly become *qualifications* if I turn them around and share them with people in a creative way.

It's such a fine line between clever and stupid.

And now to the second and final point.

I don't see myself as being in the happiness business.

In other words, not only will this book bring you no new wisdom, but it won't make you happy either. Oh, and while we're here I should take this opportunity to point out that, unlike the promise of many cheap and not so cheap weekend therapy workshops available in your area *right now*, this book is unlikely to change your life; because – that's *your* job.

Where was I?

Oh yeah, happiness.

Which, unless you hit the BIG ONE of enlightenment (and we'll explore that in the next chapter), is like all other experiences, fleeting. And I can't say that it interests me especially or even motivates me. I believe that happiness, like that other elusive delight, sex, has been harnessed by mass marketing as a sales tool, and we are made to feel somehow that if we are not in a state of perpetual bliss we are somehow falling behind or failing.

Fair enough, you look at those 1950s space age instant TV dinner smiling sexpot in a pencil skirt adverts which suggested attainment of satori if you just bought a Hoover and you can accept that in the wake of eighty million dead they might wanna be looking on the bright side... But the idea that happiness can be purchased or even that we are entitled to it is just plain dumb.

Likewise, we've somehow learned that if we are not perpetually 'in love' with our 'loved ones' then the relationship is somehow flawed, doomed or 'toxic'. Bullshit. Love is fluid, it ebbs and it flows from moment to moment, it's about as constant and consistent as the shifting oceans and to imagine that it's *predictable* is folly.

I come more from the Jim Morrison school of psychology – he

said, *"expose yourself to your deepest fear; after that, fear has no power, and the fear of freedom shrinks and vanishes. You are free."*

Not the most popular view I know, and I totally *get* that selling a book with a promise of happiness is easier and almost certainly more lucrative than one that invites and evokes your deepest fear, but don't you feel what Jim is offering is so much more *exciting*?

A great teacher of mine, the late Rex Bradley, once said to me,

emotions don't have a mixing board – they just have a master volume. You can't fade out sadness and pain and fade up happiness and joy. You turn one down they all go down.

There's a joke in Alcoholics Anonymous – there's a good thing and a bad thing about giving up drinking.

The good thing is you get your feelings back.

And the bad thing is you get your feelings back.

Likewise, if this book does happen to make you happier, it will also make you sadder. I remember going to my first therapist after the first eighteen months and saying, *"what the fuck? I feel worse now than when I first started coming,"* and she said, *"I guess it's working then."*

Happiness, like sadness and everything else in the universe, is fleeting, it comes and it goes. And also happiness is NOT a universal experience – what makes me happy certainly won't make everyone happy, so how can you write a book or a doctrine based on that one?

I only just started reading *I Am That* by Sri Nisargadatta Maharaj but on opening it the first chapter heading I saw was *All Search for Happiness is Misery*.

So I guess I'm not the first...

For me happiness is Merry Clayton's vocal on *Gimme Shelter*, the opening chord to *Hard Day's Night*, the crackle of the needle on vinyl, my daughters at the school gates, a Don McCullin photograph, a pair of vintage Mission speakers, a whole day to myself, a pair of 1947 Levis Vintage Clothing 501s, it's that almost tearful welling up of warm emotion in the heart on seeing (from my middle-class middle-aged armchair at home) the Arctic Monkeys headline Glastonbury for the first time all wide-eyed and unbelieving and grateful...

Sadness is a Cormac McCarthy book, a Don McCullin photograph, tears on my daughter's cheek as I say goodbye, an Edward Thomas poem, loneliness, everyone I've ever disappointed, absent friends, making the same fucking mistake for the hundredth time, my Grandparents' ashes in the bottom of a cupboard in the back bedroom, electricity pylons across open countryside...

It's Mumford and Sons headlining Glastonbury.

Again.

* * *

Meet yourself as a child and share your most important message.

Never obey anyone's command unless it is coming from within you also.

Celebrate your difference and recognise you belong.

Find a teacher who's lived.

Learn to value pain and pleasure equally.

Live a life true to yourself, not the life others expect of you.

Chapter 2

Hit Your Thumb Repeatedly with a 20 oz Estwing Surestrike All Steel Straight Claw Hammer...

Being an intellectual creates a lot of questions and no answers.
Janis Joplin said that...

Emotions are the windows of the soul; they are the coloured glass through which the soul sees the world. Partial illumination – partial perception. There is nothing so clear and nothing more deceptive than emotions.
George Gurdjieff said that...

The most important kind of freedom is to be what you really are. You trade in your reality for a role. You give up your ability to feel, and in exchange, put on a mask.
Jim Morrison said that...

It's okay to eat fish because they don't have any feelings.
Kurt Cobain said that...

So, we've already begun to look at emotions, but I want to ramp things up by setting the bench even higher.

Enlightenment.

Whoa... So *soon* I hear you say?

Yeah baby.

AKA self-actualisation, self-realisation, Nirvana, Kensho, Satori, Bodhi, āśraya parāvṛtti – all terms used to describe a state of *awakening* where the Mind returns to its original condition of non-attachment, non-discrimination and non-duality

A kind of throwaway term in our culture, not one that really has a place within our Western belief systems or that many people are even searching for.

But...

Why not? Why not go for the big one? I mean, what are we doing here otherwise? I've already dropped the bummer on you that this book ain't gonna teach you nuttin new or make you happy so what the heck, let's go balls out for that great cosmic cum shot...

Up for it?

Hell yeah.

Okay, but first we gotta go back to basics so come with me now, to a tropical island in a far off land...

"We really lost the war! How could they have been so sloppy?

Suddenly everything went black. A storm raged inside me. I felt like a fool – what had I been doing for all these years?

Gradually the storm subsided, and for the first time I really understood: my thirty years as a guerrilla fighter for the Japanese army were abruptly finished. This was the end.

I pulled back the bolt on my rifle and unloaded the bullets..."

Lt. Hiroo Onoda of the Imperial Japanese Army's response to hearing, in March 1972, that the war had ended and he no longer needed to defend the Philippine island of Lubang.

Doh...

Ha ha ha ha ha ha!

What a twat.

Ha ha ha ha ha ha! Ha ha ha ha ha ha!

What a fucking *doofus!*

Wouldn't you say? Taking pot shots at passing 747s when everyone else had clocked off and gone home?

What a complete and utter loser.

But, interestingly enough, that's *not* how the Japanese government responded. 'Cos they knew that if he went home and people went, *'dude? War ended like... years ago man? What the fuck?'* the poor guy would just capsize, his psyche would implode.

So you know what they did?

They gave him a hero's welcome. The whole ticker tape thing and, *in public*, they said *'thank you, thank you for carrying out your duty to the Emperor, for your loyalty to your nation, for all that you have done, now go home and live in peace with your country's blessing and eternal gratitude.'*

Made me cry when I first heard that.

The sensitivity, the awareness, the understanding of how delicate and fragile that man would be to that most intolerable of all human feelings – humiliation.

Again, my great teacher and therapist Rex Bradley showed me something once that was truly shocking. It was a Victorian guide to raising children, what would now be called a 'parenting guide.' It said:

Don't beat your children.

Which seemed quite reasonable. Forward-thinking even. But it went on. It said:

Don't beat your children – they will soon get used to it. If you want to really control them, humiliate them – preferably in public.

Cunts.

Sorry, *sorry,* but *really,* just how twisted is that? Especially the bit about doing it in *public*.

But you see they understood something fundamental about human psychology, and we're not just talking kids here. Human beings simply cannot tolerate humiliation. The US government knew that one too when they set up Guantanamo where male prisoners were not only tortured but subjected to sexual and cultural humiliation such as being paraded naked in front of female soldiers, being forced to wear women's underwear and dance with other men, being forced to watch pornography, being smeared in menstrual blood and having the Koran urinated on in front of them.

Cunts.

Sorry, *sorry*, done it again, but *really*, just how twisted is that? Especially that bit about… actually – *all* of it.

And when I worked in domestic violence it was much the same. We'd spend months getting these guys to stop beating up their women and then the complaints would come in:

> *It's even worse now. At least when he used to beat me up there'd be a few days or weeks after when he'd feel guilty and be all nice to me. Now he's just horrible all the time.*

Which is not to minimise the violence but to illustrate how utterly demoralising humiliation can be.

So how does this spiel relate to the title of this chapter?

And more importantly, how does the title of this chapter relate to enlightenment?

Well, the opposite of awakening is unconsciousness, and humiliation is one, but by no means all, of the primary reasons why people shut down and learn to ignore themselves, which makes about as much sense as hitting your thumb repeatedly with a 20 oz Estwing Surestrike all steel straight claw hammer…

Huh? No, it's true, it's a fantastic system – the pain generated

by hitting your thumb with a hammer transmits *very fucking*

quickly the information to your brain that it's probably a

really good idea to stop doing it and seek medical attention *immediately*.

Emotional pain has the very same function and transmits

more or less the same information – something hurts, something needs attending to, something's not right, something needs healing – and yet culturally we are more inclined to ignore the message, resulting in a broken and septic psyche.

Which, putting it clinically, is bonkers.

But somehow we've developed a society where it's relatively okay to attend to yourself if physically injured, albeit with the least amount of fuss as possible, but if you're wounded *emotionally* then that's really not cool – best shrug it off and pretend nothing happened if at all possible. If you break a leg and end up in hospital people might visit, bring you grapes and flowers. Bottle your emotions up until you have a breakdown and end up in a psychiatric ward and... as often as not it becomes a shameful family secret.

This applies to men *and* women although there are some gender differences, for instance with anger. Anger is a big no no for women – if a woman gets angry she's a *'crazy bitch'* or it must be *'her time of the month'*, said with a knowing look and a wry smile. She *is*, however, allowed to cry, just a few tears mind, to be dabbed away from the corner of the eye with a fine lace hankie.

(Note – my girlfriend just read this and said, *"what the fuck? How come you can write this like you know all about it and yet you hate it when I get angry?"* The simple answer is a) She hasn't read the bit where I admit to being really fucked up and b) No matter how evolved I attempt to be I, like *many* men, find women's anger repulsive and scary and I wish she'd just cry a bit and dab it away with a fine lace hanky and go back to being *nice*).

Anger for men on the other hand is obligatory – if you want to be a *man* that is. My father told me explicitly that if anyone upset me I should just punch them straight in the face. Crying, on the other hand, is expressly forbidden at all times, and should it occur will be taken as clear indication that you are homosexual.

And so we are all taught very early on to ignore painful experiences; which is a great way to prolong them. Back to the analogy – say you did hit your thumb with a hammer, but decided to ignore it. What might have been a fairly straight-forward situation if you'd treated the injury with a plaster or bandage now becomes far more complex with an even more painful and now infected thumb.

The same goes for emotion, because pain, *painful* though it is, is designed to draw your attention to an urgent situation. Ignore pain and it quickly becomes suffering, which to be quite frank, sucks.

I started with humiliation because it's intolerable. But because we have such a downer on emotions in general anything at all uncomfortable tends to get ignored.

We're at it right from the beginning with books and programmes that teach you how to ignore your baby's screams in order that you can train him or her to sleep 'properly'. Now don't get me wrong, I really get that dilemma, I've got two children, and it's a personal thing that depends on your lifestyle, but I never managed to do the ignoring thing because much as I wanted them to sleep, so that *I* could sleep, I didn't want to be part of that system of teaching them to switch off.

I remember people really hassling me to just let them cry, and eventually I went to one of my trainers and asked him what he thought. He said, *"you can ignore them and they'll soon learn to shut up, and they'll grow up socially well-adjusted people. Or you can respond to them and they'll grow up having a good relationship to themselves."*

Now to me you can learn manners later on pretty damned easily, but learning self-contact is a really hard thing to do if you leave it 'til you're older.

No brainer then.

Okay, so we've established that humiliation is utterly intol-erable, and that once you start shutting down one experience you're on the slippery slope to inner deadness. But there are so many other things, so many other ways, to shut down, to distance, to deaden, to continue the insanity, and I don't use that word lightly. I mean – we're born with this *flawless* system, an incredibly delicate, subtle and hyper sensitive and amazingly effective radar that instantly tells us what is right for us – more eloquent terms for this are intuition, instinct, listening to your gut or knowing yourself – and we spend the rest of our lives shutting it down. It's like wandering around your house switching off all the smoke alarms...

We have so many systems to assist this shutdown in our culture, alcohol, tobacco, drugs, television, pre-fab pop bands, fashion fascism, Facebook, computer games, pornography – and that's just the kids.

As Bill Hicks observed:

I think it's interesting the two drugs that are legal – alcohol and cigarettes, two drugs that do absolutely nothing for you at all – are legal, and the drugs that might open your mind up to realise how you're being fucked every day of your life, those drugs are against the law. Coincidence?

Now I'm not one for conspiracy theories even though my personal stance is that the Warren Commission was a total whitewash; Marilyn Monroe, Brian Jones, Jimi Hendrix and Kurt Cobain were probably murdered; Princess Diana was assassinated; 9/11 was an inside job; Nazi leader Martin Bormann never died and has built a global empire involving, among many others, the Bush family who are also shape-shifting alien reptiles and that there is a New World Order of shadowy elites primarily involving the owners of the private banks in the Federal Reserve System and other central banks, plus members of the Council on Foreign Relations who control and manipulate governments, industry, and media organisations worldwide and who have funded and in some cases *caused* most of the major wars of the last two hundred years, carrying out false flag attacks to manipulate populations into supporting them, and deliberately causing economic inflation and depressions at will in order to create a one-world government through which they could exert absolute dominance over the Earth and eliminate all sources of dissent.

But that's just me.

And I make no apology for quoting Bill Hicks repeatedly throughout this book, a man who if I had to choose would be my number one teacher and guru and who I regard as a true prophet, who was condemned and crucified by David Letterman and who died in his thirty-third year. Coincidence?

I don't believe so.

Bill was a very enlightened man, a true genius who used his brilliant and savage style, enhanced by 'heroic' doses of psilocybin mushrooms, to illuminate the multitude of ways that we choose to stay unconscious:

> *Go back to bed, America. Your government has figured out how it all transpired. Go back to bed, America. Your government is in control again. Here – here's American Gladiators. Watch this, shut up. Go back to bed, America. Here is American Gladiators. Here is 56 channels of it! Watch these pituitary retards bang their fucking skulls together and congratulate you on living in the land of freedom. Here you go, America! You are free to do what we tell you! You are free to do what we tell you!*

It's an amazing thing when you begin to look at it – that there is actually very little within our Western world that encourages us to really be alive, to be aware, to be conscious.

Hitting your thumb with a hammer will do it, but it's a little drastic, even for me.

So how to wake up?

This is much harder – it's always easier to learn than unlearn – and demands a much deeper exploration, requiring us to look at Mind, Body & Spirit. I was never a fan of the term and I've never really embraced much of what is now called the New Age Movement, but as a model it has its uses.

Mind.

Body.

Spirit.

Okay, so let's start with the Mind, the great God of thought, of intellect and cognition, so highly prized, so revered, so worshipped. As we well know, this is the principle aim of schooling, to impart knowledge, to train the mind, to broaden the intellect, to learn the skills of debating and rhetoric, of mathematics and grammar, to prepare one for the world of business, commerce, literature and science. And fair enough, by and large it does a good job and in this moment as I sit in front of my computer the skills I learned in reading and writing are much appreciated.

Next, the Body, the Adonis, the sportsman, the soldier, the hero, toned and shaped on the playing fields of our youth; presented to us in all its photoshopped perfection on the top, bottom and now middle shelves of every newsagent in the land; used to sell anything and everything from Coke to couture, fragrance to fish fingers, confectionary to cars and David and Victoria Beckham's fucking *pants*.

Now I don't have a sporting bone in my body. At school, my attitude whilst slogging, in totally inappropriate and ineffective attire, around the fucking *swamp* of a sports field that they insisted on using for 'games' was – you want the ball that badly? Take it man, just leave me alone and stop *threatening* me... (Whoever thought up the term *games* for the brutal and vicious gladiatorial throwback activities that occurred in that bog has obviously never encountered the British climate – in years to come the perfectly preserved corpses of youths wearing blue flannel shorts and stripy tops will be disinterred from the playing fields of Eton.)

And so finally, to the Spirit, the soul, our true selves, our essence which in school we explore by… er… which in school we develop our true nature by… hold on, I need to Google this one, I've strangely gone blank. Ah, here it is, everything I ever learned in school about my spirit:

Zip

Er... yeah, someone seemed to *forget* that lesson, unless you count singing *All Things Bright and Beautiful*. No, any kind of imparting of genuine spiritual wisdom seemed to be glaringly absent from my extremely expensive private education, hold on, let me phone a friend – no, apparently it wasn't included in State education either.

And when I say Spirit I'm not talking about God here, I'm talking about YOU, your true nature, your own deep connection to yourself and the world in which you live which makes it *really* worth repeating Gurdjieff at this point:

> *People live in a state of a hypnotic "waking sleep". Maleficent events such as wars and so on could not possibly take place if people were more awake. People in their typical state function as unconscious automatons, but one can "wake up" and become a different sort of human being altogether.*

Fact is, somewhere way *way* back in our history, even before emotions became illegal, we lost touch with our spirit, we became city dwellers and farmers and industrialists and our intuitive soulful side became redundant.

And we forgot ourselves.

As someone wise – probably Eckhart Tolle – pointed out, we are *lost in thought*.

I was twenty-six when I first discovered George Ivanovich Gurdjieff. Passing through Bombay, the only book I could find in English was Colin Wilson's *The Occult* in which there was a chapter on the great mystic. I was an addict at the time but even so I recognised immediately the description of man as an automaton, I could *feel* the experience, as if looking at the world through a plate glass window, my senses numbed by more than narcotics. And so it was a vast disappointment when I finally quit, two years down the line, and discovered that I was still stoned. I mean *shit*, what had I been wasting all my money on for all those years?

With all addiction the most important step on the way to recovery is Step One of the Twelve Step Program, *"we admitted we were powerless over alcohol/drugs/sex/love/food etc. and that our lives had become unmanageable,"* or in other words that you *wake up* to the fact that you've got a problem.

Gurdjieff made the parallel statement, *"working on oneself is not so difficult as wishing to work, taking the decision."* He drew the analogy that *"if a man in prison was at any time to have a chance of escape, then he must first of all realize that he is in prison. So long as he fails to realize this, so long as he thinks he is free, he has no chance whatever."*

Now that is a really, *really* important analogy. I promise not to repeat myself too often in this book but this time it's worth it:

> *If a man in prison*
> *was at any time to have a chance of escape,*
> *then he must first of all realize*
> *that he is in prison.*
> *So long as he fails to realize this,*
> *so long as he thinks he is free,*
> *he has no chance*
> *whatever."*

Discovering Gurdjieff did more than just set me on the road to recovery from addiction, it opened me up to the notion that I was living life in a state of sleep. *That* really blew my mind.

And what's sad is that the guy only died in 1949 and yet just over sixty years later I say to people, 'have you heard of Gurdjieff?' and nine times out of ten the answer is no. On the tenth occasion the answer is always, "fuck yeah! He's *amazing…*'

As I said, there's no new wisdom in this book, but in case you're one of the nine who don't know his work, it's worth sketching out. Gurdjieff argued that contemporary religions and spiritual traditions had lost their way, or even worse, become bastardised systems of control and manipulation. Within this spiritual void people were becoming more and more like automatons, susceptible to control from outside and increasingly capable of otherwise unthinkable acts of mass psychosis such as the wars and atrocities of the twentieth century.

Having studied extensively in the East, he returned with an understanding that many of the ancient contemplative methods of the Orient simply did not work for the Western psyche, and thus developed what he called the Fourth Way, a process tailored to the requirements and attitudes of the Western mind. The Fourth Way favoured practices such as repetitive, tedious manual labour in recognition that it was easier for the Western mind to slip into a meditative state than via more traditional disciplines.

On one occasion a disciple approached Gurdjieff and asked to be shown the secrets of the Fourth Way. Gurdjieff famously told the man to go and dig a hole. When the disciple returned having completed the task Gurdjieff told him to go and fill it in again. The disciple grew impatient and again asked to receive the teachings. Gurdjieff told him to go and dig another hole. And so on, until the disciple finally gave up asking and slipped into a meditative state.

Try it; you can do it with any menial task like doing the dishes. Clean the crockery like your life depends on it ('cos it does), with absolute focus and attention to the job in hand, total dedication and with minimal distraction. You're unlikely to become instantly enlightened but the otherwise tedious job may well take on a whole new meaning and with enough practise you just might begin to start experiencing *yourself* more fully.

Hey – no one said this was gonna be easy. In fact this term that is bandied around the therapy world so often of 'working on oneself' was originally coined by Gurdjieff and has more recently come to describe all personal growth. He called it that because that is what's required – hard work.

And shit – we've got it easy with our attempts at spiritual evolution, that Bikram yoga class or reiki training is nothing compared to what many cultures endure, they even make Gurdjieff look lightweight. The Lakota used an initiation ritual called the Vision Quest, requiring four days to be spent alone in the wilderness without food, water or sleep. They also practiced the Sun Dance where the men's chests were pierced with ropes that were attached to a tree, which they then danced around until they tore free.

Even more mental are the still existing 'marathon monks of Mt. Hiei' in Japan. They endure a thousand-day practice known as Kaihōgyō, which requires them to run (at night – you wouldn't want it to be too *easy*) a thirty-kilometre run every day for a hundred days, for five consecutive years. It gets worse. During the sixth year they complete one hundred *sixty*-kilometre runs. At the end of this they then spend nine days without food, water or sleep.

When running they wear thin pyjamas, sandals and carry a short sword known as a tantō. And you just know what that tantō is for don'tcha? The mountain path along which they run is littered with the graves of monks who have fulfilled the pledge to take their own lives should they fail, only forty-six having completed the challenge since 1585.

Now I'm not knocking the transcendental meditation technique that you perfected during that weekend workshop in Kentish Town, I'm just saying, no one ever committed hara-kiri for losing focus whilst doing the dishes…

Fortunately for me I discovered Gurdjieff's approach immediately prior to working as a stage hand on a TV music show called *The White Room* which required me to paint the whole of Docklands Arena in four coats of white emulsion. Ten days of white on white on white on white and not once did I consider ritual disembowelment…

The Fourth Way was designed to work on all three aspects of

the human being, Mind, Body *and* Spirit, primarily through a technique known as *self-remembering,* designed to increase and focus people's attention and energy to minimize the daydreaming and absentmindedness that results in unconscious automation. As with Hicks and Osho (a great fan of Gurdjieff), he challenged ideas of religion, personality and morality, saying that these conventions were designed to make it possible for people not to have to think for themselves.

Most of Gurdjieff's books are deliberately impenetrable, but his student P.D. Ouspensky is an easier read (see *In Search of the Miraculous*). Here he describes his initial struggle with self-remembering:

The very first attempts showed me how difficult it was. Attempts at self-remembering failed to give any results except to show me that in actual fact we never remember ourselves.' With practise however he began to notice, *'that self-remembering gave wonderful sensations which come to us only very seldom and in exceptional conditions. I used to like to wander through St. Petersburg at night and to 'sense' the houses and the streets. St. Petersburg is full of these strange sensations. Houses, especially old houses, were quite alive, I all but spoke to them. There was no 'imagination' in it. I did not think of anything, I simply walked along while trying to remember myself and looked about; the sensations came by themselves.*

Osho too talked often of self-remembering. In his book *Tantra – The Supreme Understanding* he says:

Keep your wristwatch before you, and look at the hand that shows seconds and remember only one thing: "I am looking at the hand which is showing seconds." *You will not be able to remember for even three seconds together. You will forget many times... just a simple thing:* "I am looking and I will remember this; that I am looking."

You will forget. Many things will come into your mind. You have made an appointment; just looking at the watch the association will come into the mind: "I have to go at five o'clock to meet a friend." Suddenly the thought comes and you have forgotten that you are looking at it. Just by looking at the watch you may start thinking of Switzerland because it is Swiss-made. But you will not be able to remember; even for three consecutive seconds that you are looking at the hand showing seconds moving.

If you can attain to one minute's self-remembering, I promise to make you a Buddha.

You can observe your sleep state quite easily. How many times today did you forget yourself? Driving across town – do you remember changing gear? Indicating? Accelerating? Probably not, unless you're a beginner. When you start driving you're super conscious of every manoeuvre, of every action. A few months down the line and you can drive the length of the country without being conscious of yourself and what you're doing for one moment.

And how many times have you heard people describe an experience of crisis or emergency as time slowing down and becoming ultra lucid? These intense events like car crashes and disasters are when we suddenly become super aware. *This* is the function of self-remembering, to experience yourself as your own person, beyond ego, beyond personality, but preferably without the crisis.

Here is a simple Gurdjieff technique for self-remembering that you can practice almost anywhere, any time.

Close your eyes. Go inside. Place your awareness on yourself. Absolutely. Fully experience yourself as deeply as possible, your heartbeat, your breath, your thoughts, there's no need to change anything – just *observe*.

Now open your eyes. Take a breath and place your awareness on the outside, on your environment, your surroundings, everything that's external – just *observe*.

And now – do both. *Fully* experience your inner and outer world simultaneously.

Got it?

No, me neither. Maybe for a second… but, it's a bastard. This is why sadhus sleep on beds of nails. Gurdjieff would probably approve of the hammer-thumb approach to enlightenment – it's hard being conscious, incredibly hard, and the odds are against us.

But don't worry, don't be disheartened – just keep practising it.

Tell yourself as many times as possible every day to wake up. Cover your house with post-it notes, or my preferred approach, get a tattoo. Do whatever you need to do to remind yourself at every possible opportunity and do it…

For the rest of your life.

* * *

Begin to entertain the notion of enlightenment.

Learn to respect and listen to all pain.

Observe and recognise your sleep state during your daily routine.

Self-remembering is a highly advanced technique – practice it for one second at a time and don't be disheartened if you find it difficult; persevere.

Chapter 3

How to Polish a Turd...

Comfort zones are plush lined coffins. When you stay in your plush lined coffins, you die.
Stan Dale said that...

If you look for truth, you may find comfort in the end; if you look for comfort you will not get either comfort or truth only soft soap and wishful thinking to begin, and in the end, despair.
C.S. Lewis said that...

The superior man thinks always of virtue; the common man thinks of comfort.
Confucius said that...

This new learning amazes me, Sir Bedevere. Explain again how sheep's bladders may be employed to prevent earth-quakes.
King Arthur said that...

The Guest House by Jalal al-din Rumi

This being human is a guest house. Every morning a new arrival. A joy, a depression, a meanness, some momentary awareness comes as an unexpected visitor. Welcome and entertain them all. Even if they're a crowd of sorrows, who violently sweep your house empty of its furniture, still treat each guest honorably. He may be clearing you out for some new delight. The dark thought, the shame, the malice, meet them at the door laughing, and invite them in. Be grateful for whoever comes, because each has been sent as a guide from beyond.

Here's how the Grail Quest was told to me. The scholars among you might – quite rightly – think, hold on, this isn't the Grail story as I know it, to which I say – it's a *myth*. It never *happened*. But this version was told to me by somatic therapy pioneer Stanley Keleman, friend and colleague of the great mythologist Joseph Campbell – and that's good enough for me.

So… the Knights of the Round Table were comfortably ensconced in Camelot, growing fat and lazy and predictable. And lo, they were presented with a vision of the Holy Grail and so set forth on a heroic quest in search of the mystical chalice.

In doing so they had to leave the safety of Camelot and enter the Wasteland. The Wasteland sucked, it was a bleak and inhospitable terrain with little sustenance or vegetation, much like London Docklands when I squatted there in '84. Once they crossed the Wasteland – and not all of them made it – they had to enter the Forest. The Forest was wild and overgrown and they were beset on all sides by dragons and demons and trolls and evil spirits and temptresses. In order to penetrate the Forest they were not permitted to take an existing path, for to take an existing path was to take another's path. No, the Knights had to cut their own path through the dense thorny undergrowth and they received many a scrape, scratch and itchy rash to which some of the Knights succumbed.

The hero of this particular Grail story was Sir Percival, an innocent knight whose name means simple fool. Sir Percy quested far and wide for five long and lonely years, at times falling prey to the challenges and temptations of the path but ultimately returning to the Quest. At length he came to an isolated and spooky castle, and therein resided the Fisher King – the Grail Keeper.

The Fisher King was ailing from a horrendous wound (actually he'd been shot through the balls by an arrow – but that's a *whole* other metaphor…), he was old and weak and frail. Sir Percy was so driven by his search for the Grail that he made no mention of the Fisher King's injury, to which the Fisher King responded by thinking – fuck you, I'm not gonna tell you that I've got the Grail hidden up in my attic. And so, the next morning, Sir Percy was sent out from the castle and returned once again to his Quest.

Five more years passed, and again Sir Percy wandered fruitlessly and alone throughout the inhospitable land as he faced many more adventures and challenges than we have time to go into here and now.

At length he came upon a Dark Knight (he was his half-brother or summink, the detail escapes me). A mighty battle ensued, they fought valiantly for many hours until eventually the Dark Knight smote Sir Percival's sword with such a blow that it cleft in twain (snapped in half). Our hero lay defenceless and exhausted on the ground.

"Yield," the Dark Knight commanded, as was the chivalrous tradition.

"*Never*," Sir Percy replied, for his pride was too great.

The Dark Knight raised his sword to dispatch our fallen hero. But as he did so, a change came upon him and he lowered his blade and extended his hand.

"Arise Sir Knight," he said. "You have been a worthy opponent and – I dunno... it just doesn't seem *right* to kill you now that you lay there in the dirt with no weapon with which to defend yourself."

Sir Percival arose and in that moment he too was transformed. Not only was he given his life, but also he experienced – for the first time ever – the *compassion* of another.

He rode forth and in time came once again to the Fisher King's castle. The drawbridge was lowered and the minute he entered and saw the Grail Keeper he said, "My Lord, what ails thee?"

In that moment the Holy Grail was revealed to him, for, as you may or may not know, the Holy Grail represents compassion, and as he reached for the chalice, it vanished, for he now had it within himself.

Which was nice.

Joseph Campbell was asked why, with the multitude of myths and stories that have been lost or forgotten, does the Arthurian legend endure. He explained that it's because it has contemporary relevance in the sense that it represents the therapeutic journey – the awakening and call to a quest, the leaving of the comfort zone of what is familiar, the venturing forth into the wasteland and forests of the unknown, the challenges, temptations, successes and failures along the way, and ultimately, for the committed, the Holy Grail of therapy. Self/compassion.

"But hold on a minute", you'd be forgiven for thinking. *"One minute he's going on about enlightenment, next he's gone all King Arthur. What's the link? And why leave Camelot?"*

Fair enough, but there are two very important things you need on the road to enlightenment. The first is self-compassion, and the second is the willingness to leave the comfort zone – remember those crazy running monks – especially when our cultural value systems do *so* encourage us to raise the drawbridge and hunker down inside. Just about everything that we do, that we aspire to, that we are *driven* by is the desire to achieve comfort and security. Central heating, air conditioning, double glazing, home delivery shopping, health insurance, home insurance, life insurance, indemnity insurance, travel insurance, *pet* insurance, pension schemes, savings plans, age concern personal alarm services, anti-virus software, security systems, chip and pin fraud prevention, monitored home alarm systems with key-holders and police response, CCTV installation for home or small business from £699, night vision security cameras attached to motion detecting digital video recorders, panic rooms constructed with reinforced steel sheeting, eight-inch concrete walls, steel doors, special locking systems and soundproofing…

But have you noticed, that the more of this shit you surround yourself with, the more *scared* you feel?

And *that's* why we should all leave Camelot, because the truth is, it's a lunatic asylum masquerading as a safe haven. Consider the fact that when people are deemed too dangerous to be part of society we consign them to *secure* units. The comfort zone is a place of deep sleep, of putrefaction, a cotton wool existence where time passes unnoticed until one day you open your eyes and wonder where your life went, or as Paolo Coelho put it in *The Pilgrimage*, it's a perpetual Sunday afternoon existence.

Then again, trying to promote life beyond *the zone* is a hard sell. As a society alienated from most notions of self-actualization and indoctrinated in the principles of right and wrong, good and bad, it's very hard to give value to discomfort and struggle, but like the Knights in the Wasteland, it's where you come alive, where you test your mettle, where you become whole. Or, as Martin Luther King said, *"the ultimate measure of a man is not where he stands in moments of comfort and convenience, but where he stands at times of challenge and controversy."*

Consider the things that have changed you. Were they easy? Were they *pain free*?

One of the biggest things that changed me was going to India as a twenty something white boy from the Slough Windsor borders and finding myself in the Middle Ages where all the rules I knew clearly did not apply. Fog-bound on a high speed bus driven by someone whose driving style suggested a definite belief in reincarnation, I encountered death for the first time. A car packed with young school children had collided head on with a large truck and they lay strewn all over the road in awkward poses, blood staining their smart school uniforms.

Indians scattered on dawn's highway, bleeding
Ghosts crowd the young child's fragile eggshell mind...

It smacked me in the face like a self-conscious Jim Morrison poem and something in me changed forever, I awoke to the fact that in the West we deny death by clearing it away in nice white vans before anyone can see it and realise that we are not, in fact, immortal.

Of course, if you're committed to *the zone* then every problem is seen as a disaster, a failure, a catastrophe. Value life beyond *the zone* and each challenge becomes a qualification or, as it's known in the trade, an AFGO.

Another fuckin' growth opportunity.

Ok, now would seem a good time to talk shit for a while.

Shit. One of the most popular words in the Western language. Hey man – this is good shit. I couldn't give a shit. I'm really in the shit. Shit happens. You're shitting me. That's some fucked-up shit. We love it, it slides off the tongue so easily, it can be interjected almost limitlessly into just about any phrase or sentence, but – when it 'happens' to us...

WE FUCKING HATE IT.

Oh we *hate* being in the shit, we'll do just about anything to avoid it, to stay in *the zone*.

But, embrace The Church of AFGO and suddenly you'll notice that in every lump of shit there are diamonds to be found. Sometimes you have to pull a turd to pieces bit by bit with your naked fingers to find them but somewhere in that warm, claggy, stinking dung, if you dig deep enough, they'll be there. Sometimes they're small, almost insignificant, half-carat uncut stones, at other times you might be fortunate enough to unearth a giant Princess-shaped sparkler, but if you walk away with your nose covered and your face screwed up in disgust you'll miss the greatest riches of all, the shit-stained gems of self-knowledge and growth.

Which is why I'd like to suggest that you never go anywhere without a carrier bag...

And no – this isn't stage two (stage one was convincing you that you're a Gonzo seeker) of my secret plan to become Cult Leader and Grand Wizard of The Church of AFGO and persuade you, once you've slept with me, denounced your family and signed over your entire estate to a shady figure known to you only as *The Rector,* (Arab Bank (Switzerland) Ltd, Sort Code 33 47 96, Account Number 11685849) that all will be well and we will ascend as one and in eternal unity to the Mother Ship by simply wearing a Tesco's bag over your head (I'll be joining you later) and drinking one of my delicious aspirin smoothies...

Honest.

Trust me.

When I was a kid my grandmother, Alice, and I would spend days exploring the fertile landscape of Buckinghamshire. We'd set out in the morning with our walking sticks, a hunk of bread and cheese, and most important of all, a carrier bag. And as we strolled we'd gather horseshit, returning home late in the day with our precious sack of brown fibrous truffles, which Alice would inter at the feet of her tomato plants. In time, through some unseen alchemical transformation, sweet and succulent fruit would blossom in such abundance that we knew not what to do with the bastard things by mid August...

But it taught me the value of shit. Magical fertilising matter packed with nutrients, full of growth and life and vigour – need I go on? You're feeling the metaphor right?

Life is full of shit.

Life's shit and then you die...

How about – life is fertile and abundant with the opportunity to grow – and then you die anyway.

Same thing, depending on your outlook. Best way I know to have an utterly miserable life is to view the shit we encounter as *bad.* Someone sent me a quote by Zen master, Shunryu Suzuki, who when asked what the secret of his spirituality was, responded, *"I truly don't care what happens next."* Now there's a man who's found enlightenment through not caring if he steps in dog shit, and don't get me wrong, it's a tall order, but it's the right *direction.*

I'm not a fan of dogma or doctrine and I've always shied away from organised religion, but I'll tell you something – the people who, when they fall on their arses pick themselves up the quickest, are the ones who look for the growth opportunity in the situation. And the only way to really do that is to have a compassionate overview, or as the Buddha taught, observe yourself *lovingly*; otherwise you get stuck in the judgement. 'Why was I so stupid? I'm such an idiot/twat/plonker/asshole... I *really* fucked up that time...' That's the best way to feel even worse and stay in the shit, because judgement of yourself or others just shuts the whole thing down, which after all is the function of judgement. Guilty, go to jail, case closed.

And, by the way, this is really what this whole trip, this whole ride, is all about, it's about developing the art of *self-enquiry*, of knowing yourself, of observing yourself with compassion and interest – perhaps the single most important teaching I have ever received.

Observe lovingly.

Easily said, but hard to maintain – judgment belongs in the courthouse.

So in order to extract the nutrients from the fertiliser you have to suspend judgement and get interested in what just happened and that's where the *self-compassion* comes in. So next time you get a parking ticket, instead of getting furious with the traffic warden, the government, the system, *yourself*, you might wanna get interested – that's the *third* ticket I've got this month. When I think about it I realise that I'm overwhelmed; I need a break; work's getting on top of me; I need to slow down 'cos I haven't paid my credit card bill or got any food in lately or dealt with my tax and I notice that when I get behind on my admin I get stressed and take my eye off the ball and these things start to happen.

Or it may be deeper than that. I'm depressed, I haven't slept properly in weeks 'cos of the new baby, I'm not taking care of myself...

Or – I have an attitude problem with authority and I hate being told where to park and I might need to look at the roots of that 'cos this is beginning to cost me money and now I think of it, this is much wider than parking, I've been fired from my last three jobs for telling my boss to get fucked and I may need to look at how my dad used to bully me blah blah...

But tell yourself you're an idiot because you got yet another ticket and you close the whole thing down and there's nothing to be learned.

You miss the AFGO.

So...

Leave the comfort zone. That doesn't mean destroy your life, it means look at how you've become habit-bound, how you avoid taking risks, numb out through routine. As we've already explored, Gurdjieff was hot on this one, with his techniques for waking people up like getting them to wear their shoes on the wrong feet just to remember that they were alive. I'm not so hard-core – I'd suggest maybe wearing your watch on the other wrist, that way each time you look at the time you momentarily wake up to the fact that your watch isn't where it normally is, remind yourself you're here, right now, in this moment. That's a good warm-up.

Give yourself a *break*. Judgement belongs in the courthouse; get interested in yourself and *how* you do *what* you do. Observe yourself *lovingly*.

Be willing to adopt a completely different attitude to the shit that happens and renounce any attachment that you might have to an easy life. To be alive to joy you need to be alive to pain. Now, none of us wilfully avoids joy, but you shut down pain and joy drops accordingly. Remember, there's no mixing desk when it comes to emotions, just one giant master volume control, you turn one down, you turn 'em all down and next thing you know is you're living a beige existence. Trouble is you won't know it, 'cos it'll be so beige, and the danger of that is twofold. Either you'll cruise along until the end of your life with a vague sense that it *just wasn't meant to be like this.* Or one day you'll just pop, you'll unravel and fall apart and then you're in breakdown territory which, believe me, isn't any fun at all.

But at least you'll be alive...

* * *

Build and strengthen self-compassion.

Recognise and be willing to leave your comfort zone.

Learn to value the seemingly shit things – see the AFGO in every challenging situation.

Practice the art of observing yourself lovingly. All the time.

Chapter 4

Play from Your Fucking Heart...

Most people die of a sort of creeping common sense, and discover when it is too late that the only things one never regrets are one's mistakes.
Oscar Wilde said that...

Hell, there are no rules here – we're trying to accomplish something.
Thomas Eddison said that...

There are only two mistakes one can make along the road to truth; not going all the way, and not starting.
The Buddha said that...

Integrity has no need of rules.
Albert Camus said that...

F*ck political correctness, that went down with the World Trade Center.
Blackie Lawless of WASP, said that...
(And there's a certain irony that the site where I found that quote censored the word fuck.)

My first tattoo (well, that's not strictly true, my first was an Om that I had done in 1983 at Dennis Cockell's studio on the Finchley Road and I fainted) was *nothing is true, everything is permitted*, the last words of Hassan-i Sabbāh, the Old Man of the Mountain. Hassan was the founder of a sect of Ismaili Shi'i called the Hashashin, who lived in northern Iran in the eleventh century, and I could write another whole book on that lot but it's his final, confusing utterance that captivated me when I first heard it when I was seventeen.

It floated around in my head for another twenty-five years, but it wasn't until I finally left Camelot and begun to wake up that I could make sense of it. I'd thought that I'd walked out of the castle when I quit drugs and found therapy for the first time when I was twenty-eight – I ventured out into the Wasteland for a year, climbed the walls and howled and screamed as the anesthetic left my system, but the wilderness was too much for me and I soon sank back into another comfort zone, swapping rock and roll for suburbia and by the time I was in my early forties I was living a perpetual Sunday afternoon existence.

I'd married the woman of my dreams, we had a young family, I had a BMW, a five-bedroom house and my career as a therapist had been stratospheric. I had what most people would have considered a wonderful life, shit – *I* knew I had a wonderful life, the one that I'd worked hard to attain and that society said I *should* have, but inside my soul was dying – I'd lost a part of myself, I was becoming a creature of the commonplace. I had the terrible feeling that my life had become guaranteed, I could see it stretching out before me, safe and predictable, and that was when I returned to Hassan's epitaph.

I did some research and what I discovered was that rather than being an invitation to total moral *abandon*, the phrase had been taken up by William Burroughs and The Beats as a statement of artistic freedom. Nothing is true. *Everything* is permitted. Now – could Jackson Pollock or Picasso (or Damien Hurst for that matter) have done what they did without that philosophy?

And I... I realised that I didn't have to follow *the rules*; I didn't have to listen to the programming, to *Mr. Jones*...

I remember waking up one morning and having an argument with my two-year-old daughter Tara who wanted ketchup on her cereal which was not – I repeat *not* – gonna happen under *any* circumstances, resulting in screaming, shouting, tears and the slow dawning question... what have I *become*? Who really gives a fuck? She's two. It's ketchup and Cheerios. It ain't arsenic.

I had Hassan's words tattooed into my flesh, at which point things started to really unravel.

I fell in love with another woman. I walked out on my wife and children. I brought untold hurt to those I love the most.

I didn't just leave Camelot; I tore it down.

And it wasn't just any woman; it was a member of one of my creativity groups, someone who was a trainee at the therapy centre where I practiced – the most forbidden of fruits. One stolen kiss on a cold December evening was all it took to change the course of history for my great, great grandchildren and all those that come after them and many, many more.

See, something I'd always known about myself was that I would never be unfaithful. I knew it. I mean, I *knew* it. My dad had been a serial shagger so I was never gonna go down that road. Would never happen, not in a million years, would have bet my children's lives on it. Seriously.

And then I had the affair that ended my marriage.

And that's because I was arrogant enough, or forgetful enough, or asleep enough to think – unfaithful? Not me. No way – I don't even need to *consider* that one...

So it became a blind spot, and that's why it's dangerous to ignore the dark side 'cos it'll sneak up on you and bite you hard. We're gonna talk about that a lot in this book...

And so I hurled myself from the highest tower, and with the drawbridge firmly closed behind me, I remember realising – there's only one way I'm gonna get through this one, I've got to treat it as the biggest AFGO of all time...

And listen – I'm not advocating blowing yours, or anyone else's lives to pieces in the name of 'freedom', but if you do, commit to it *one hundred per cent*. Don't fuck around in a great cesspit of remorse, regret and guilt – that ain't gonna help anyone.

Looking back on it all I now see that if I *had* to do it, which in itself is debatable, there were ways I could have done it less savagely, with more care and compassion and *consciousness*. And with hindsight, could I have learned everything I've learned without destroying so much?

It's nice to think so.

But when did nice ever really mean anything? Certainly, if I'd been a more conscious person, it wouldn't have been possible to do so much harm.

"Maleficent events such as wars and so on could not possibly take place if people were more awake."

Trouble was I was *not* awake; I'd just replaced drugs for suburbia. There *was* a kind of nagging awareness like a voice from fifty feet under water that kept trying to get my attention, but at the same time my own shadow side was presenting me with a very compelling argument. Every time I attempted to do 'the right' thing it would whisper in my ear, *"you're living a life of compromise – like an ex-con trying to go straight, you're denying your rock and roll past, feigning conventionality, you don't belong here..."*

There was *some* truth to that.

But the fact is, as I walked into my self-imposed exile, I could have taken my family with me. Or, if I was choosing exile for myself, I didn't *have* to drag my lover with me into the desert... I could have spared her that; she was very damaged by my actions also – the ripple effects were felt far and wide. But... then again, maybe I had to lose everything.

Shit.

What you will find, if you live long enough, is that life...

Is fucking contradictory.

I guess, if I could do the John Williams exercise and go back seven years to give the forty-two-year-old 'me' some advice, I'd be saying, *"slow down. Slow RIGHT down. Cool your boots. This situation clearly isn't working, but...*

Chill.

Take some time to be by yourself, to reflect, to consider, think of the consequences not just for yourself but also for your wife, your kids... for her... *You can make changes without exploding.*

Do some SERIOUS work on your shadow side, on your darkness, before you make this *move, otherwise you're gonna live in that darkness for a long, long time."*

I'd say something like that.

And would I have listened?

Probably not.

But if I had listened to that, you know what I might have discovered? That I'm a cheat.

No shit, I hear you say.

No, I mean not only in my marriage, but *every* relationship I ever had. In my attempt to not be like my dad I'd buried that side of myself SO deep that I just couldn't see it. I created little stories to deny it, to keep it in the dark; *she* cheated on *me* first, we were on a *break* at the time, I was only *young*...

But it was still cheating. And it caught up with me.

Had I listened and done the work that made me realise I was a cheat, then I would have had the choice to do something different. I might have woken up to the fact that the cheating was just avoidance, a pain-relieving system that caused untold pain.

But having *not* done the work and careening blindly into the darkness, I continued to hide. *She* seduced *me*. I *tried* not to. I was *unhappy*. I'm an *artist*, I'm not made for this life of *convention*.

IT WASN'T MY FAULT. NO ONE UNDERSTANDS ME.

Bullshit.

I was out of control. I flirted, seduced and cheated without thought for my children, my wife, my lover, my family, friends or community.

Powerful, *powerful* thing the Shadow.

Back when I was in school I remember one kid whose parents

were divorced. These days it's easier than ever to blow our relationships, our families, to pieces.

Years ago, when I'd been practicing only a few months, I had a client commit suicide. I mean, you know the risks when you take the job – at some point in your career as a therapist you might have a client do that. At some point.

I'd been working three months.

That's for me to carry. But the point is, there are people walking around *alive* today because of what I learned through that experience. Does that make his death worth it? That's a kind of crass and unanswerable question.

It's just how it is.

Likewise, there are families intact today because of what I learned through destroying mine. Does that make it worth it? Not to me it fucking doesn't.

It's just how it is.

I would say that, for roughly one in every five couples I see, it's the right decision for them to split. The relationship has run its course, they are together for the wrong reasons, it's damaged beyond repair. But the other couples, if they can just ride the current situation out, they tend to stick together, they surf the wave and things calm down and they get a new lease. Bail at the first hurdle and, especially when you got kids, you've made a decision that there's no going back from, and whilst that may seem very attractive when you're sick of changing nappies and

sleepless nights and no sex and HIM or HER, it can also set you up for a lifetime of regret and pain.

For years before we split I used to have a recurring dream that I had an affair (yeah, yeah, you'd be forgiven for asking – why the *fuck* didn't you take THAT ONE to your therapist?). I'd wake up in the morning, sweating, heart beating, thinking, *'thank GOD that was just a nightmare.'* And then, once I'd gone and actually *done* it, I'd open my eyes and pinch myself and realise that I'd woken up too late this time...

It's a life sentence.

Now it's not *all* bad, the dust has settled, more or less, my children seem happy – time will tell what damage it did to them – I'm just saying look before you leap yeah? There's no way back up from that ledge so make sure it's the right decision for all. This book is supposed to fit, somewhat uncomfortably, into the *Self-Help* section, I'm not trying to create a whole new *Self-Destruct* genre.

But remember this – living apart from your children goes against NATURE. If your soul's screaming out for *authenticity! I must have* **authenticity!** just *how* authentic are you gonna feel when you're one of the *four* parents who regularly do the school run?

Okay, let's move on, but speaking of authenticity, we haven't talked about that yet, and I know that's been bugging you 'cos what spirituality book is worth the cover charge without a hefty dose of talk about authenticity?

So here goes.

Chances are if you have a dull, grey, low grade ever present depressed feeling, if you live life with a sense that something's missing, like something's not quite right, you too are probably living an inauthentic existence.

Approaching forty, I'd turned my back on rock and roll, the leather jacket was in the attic, the guitars had rusty strings, shit – my AC30 hadn't had a valve service in *years*. I was buying slacks in Paul *Smith*, that's how far gone I was.

But to understand how I'd got here you have to go even further back in time to my late twenties, a band called W.A.S.P. and their singer Blackie Lawless, to whom I owe my spiritual awakening – thank you Blackie, you changed my life.

My band had split and I was paying the rent whoring myself

out as a stage hand on music videos. And so it was that one fateful day I found myself at the foot of a stage in a rock and roll venue in Clapham, South London.

But this was no ordinary stage. No, this stage bore the weight of soft rock big hair lycra-wearing demigods W.A.S.P. and their front-man Blackie Lawless. There has been much speculation as to what the band's name means – some have suggested We Are Sexual Perverts but given that the drummer was wearing a *Fuck Iraq* T-shirt (this was during the first Gulf War) my money's on White Anglo Saxon Protestants.

My friend (ex pre-Queen Freddie Mercury guitar man) Chris Chesney and I had spent the day since the early hours constructing a gallows behind the drum riser on which, once the band were rocking at full tilt, we were to hang a beautiful young man with waist length hair who as I understand it was supposed to represent the teenage, angst-ridden Blackie.

This prospect... disturbed me.

I'm profoundly anti-capital punishment.

I'm profoundly anti-soft rock big hair lycra-wearing demigod white Anglo Saxon Protestants.

So you can understand that the combination of the two presented me with an ethical dilemma of vast proportions.

I have no memory of the grotesque song that the band were playing but I remember at the time the creeping realisation that some miserable kid in Peanut Ridge, Arkansas would be listening to it backwards sooner or later and deciding it was time to die and that my being paid to work on this utter shit meant I was in my own way party to his death.

And it was as this vision floated through my troubled psyche that Chris sidled up to me and in his own dry way muttered under his breath, *"I didn't condemn him – I merely nailed him to the cross..."* and that was it – my career in the 'film business' was over. I never set foot on a sound stage again, I had no idea what came next but I knew that if I reached the end of my life and looked back and all I'd done was promote the 'work' of dog shit like W.A.S.P. then I might as well take a dive off that gallows myself.

For the first time my still young if drug-addled soul cried out for *meaning*.

And so, ultimately, I went down the path of psychotherapy that lead to suburbia and respectability. I'd spent my twenties rebelling and now was my chance to make good, to fit in, to belong.

It's just it didn't work because I left a big part of myself behind. In my teens I became obsessed with two films – *Apocalypse Now* and *Performance*, (which is where I first heard Jagger mumbling 'nothing is true, everything is permitted'). Didn't understand either. But they got inside me. Now, thirty years later, I have a better idea of what they touched in me – the parts of me that split, the rock 'n roller and the conventional therapist.

The end of *Apocalypse Now* is shot in such a way that at times it's hard to tell Brando and Sheen apart. At the end of *Performance* Mick Jagger and James Fox famously merge. They become one, good and evil, right and wrong, dangerous and safe, black and white, they join to create…

A person.

A whole person.

As Jung said, *"do you want to be good… or whole?"*

And believe me, there's no way you're ever going to wake up unless you're willing to look at yourself as a whole, all your energy will be expended in repressing whatever darkness that lives within you – Osho went as far as saying that the darkness is only really possible when we forget ourselves.

The relief that I felt in owning my darkness was the relief of becoming more whole, the relief of forgetting less. And now, after much turmoil, I've managed to rebuild myself and this time it's a hybrid – part rock and roller, part professional therapist. As separate entities they just didn't work, but as a whole – I haven't looked back.

But for all the books expounding the virtues of authenticity I want to make an important point here – you will not be liked.

Get used to that idea – if you're gonna be authentic you're gonna *seriously* piss people off. And you're gonna piss powerful people off, people in authority, people who want you to do things their way. I don't bang on about breaking rules *just* because I'm immature and petulant; I do it because it's the only route possible if you're going to be true to yourself. Morality doesn't apply, ethics don't apply, laws don't apply – nothing is true, everything is permitted.

It takes HUGE balls and a commitment to living fearlessly with absolute integrity to exist as a truly authentic person, you're going to get into a *lot* of trouble, lose friends, make enemies, be judged and criticised – it's going to really hurt.

But you'll also experience the most wonderful sense of freedom imaginable and you won't live life as a slave or with that ever present nagging feeling that you've somehow sold out.

It's worth pointing out that my reaction to the life I was living was *not* authentic – lying and cheating never is. But the deep down feeling that I was living a lie *was*. And for the record, I believe that *this* is the reason my former wife ultimately forgave, or at least understood, my betrayal, and why we as a family, albeit in a reconstructed way, now function well.

Deep down we all instinctively respect people who live by their truth even if we don't like their actions, but the level of commitment required to be authentic is no small thing.

There are NO days off.

And, as I suggested earlier when exploring the notion of self-remembering, when people want to really commit to something they sometimes put a post-it note on the fridge. But I believe that in order to *really* change we need total, ever present commitment (this means daily practice, sorry gang, but seeing a therapist once a week isn't enough, that weekend workshop that promises life-changing results *isn't enough*. Growth... is a lifestyle).

And so I say – stop messing around, post-it notes are for pussies.

Go see my man Darryl at Diamond Jack's and get a tattoo (and please – might I suggest something a little more *meaningful* than a butterfly sticking out of your arse-crack?)

One of the tricks I employ when I'm struggling with the commitment that an AFGO requires is, I remind myself – *I wrote this...*

There's a Buddhist belief that before you incarnated this time round your soul sat down and wrote the whole script to your life. You wrote *what* was gonna happen, *how* it was gonna happen, who your parents were and what they were like, the different events that would occur, the people you'd meet, the partners who would love you and leave you, *the shit that would occur.*

The whole caboodle.

Now I'm not saying I believe in that *literally*. But I believe in it. Totally. It helps me stay responsible, keeps me from feeling like a victim, stops me complaining about my lot, and as long as I don't think about it too much, it helps.

As long as I don't get lost in thought.

'Cos as we already established, it doesn't do to think too much, to over use the Mind, to ask *why*. In fact it's dangerous – as a friend of mine said recently, the Mind is a wonderful servant, but a terrible master... Here's a story that illustrates this well, about the Australian Aborigines.

The Aborigines relied – *relied* – on telepathy to communicate, much like we do with our mobile phones, across vast expanses of the outback. For thousands of years.

Then the white settlers showed up and went – *nah – that doesn't make sense, you can't do that.*

And the Aborigines considered this and went – *well, y'know what, now you* think *about it, it doesn't really make sense does it?*

And they lost the ability.

They thought about it. And it died.

Thought. The killer of magic.

Now I'm not knocking it – well, I *am*, but not totally, I just mean, shit... we kinda over-did it with the whole thinking trip y'know. Ok, it's got its uses but it kills the *magic*.

Santa Claus.

Fairies.

God.

They just *can't* exist.

FUCK.

When the world makes sense, inner sense dies. What a price to pay for cleverness.

Anyway, back to the clinical shit:

Ectomorph.

Endomorph.

Mesomorph.

Ancient Greek words see? That means they're clever. Let's see what Wikipedia has to say about it:

Somatype constitutional psychology is a theory, developed in the 1940s by American psychologist William Herbert Sheldon, associating body types with human temperament types. Sheldon's 'somatotypes' are as follows:

- Ectomorphic: characterized by long and thin muscles/limbs with low fat storage; usually referred to as slim.
- Mesomorphic: characterized by medium bones, solid torso, low fat levels, wide shoulders with a narrow waist.
- Endomorphic: characterized by increased fat storage, a wide waist and a large bone structure.

The idea that these general body-types may correlate with general psychological types did not originate with Sheldon. In general outline, it resembles ideas found, for instance, in the tridosha system of Ayurveda and propounded in the twentieth century by George Gurdjieff. Sheldon's ideas may also owe something to Aristotle's conception of the soul.

Phew…

Whatevs.

I was in a somatic study group for years– along with a great many others I suspect – pretending that I knew what the hell was being talked about. Was all Greek to me, until someone in the class said, "it's simple – it's just thinker, doer, feeler."

Well why the *fuck* didn't someone say that, years ago? That's *simple*. So, I get it, there are *three* constitutional types of people – those whose primary tendency is to *think*, those who are *action* oriented – who *do*, and those who *feel*.

Now in Western society our system tends to value thinkers, intellectuals, over all else, even to the extreme that this is reflected in the type of people who become catwalk models – *ectomorphic: characterized by long and thin muscles/limbs and low fat storage; usually referred to as slim.* Were our systems more Eastern in valuing emotions one might suppose that there would be some right chubby feeling-full endomorphs wobbling down the catwalk like graceful Buddhas.

There *is* a valuing of doers, of mesomorphs – the Bruce Willises or Marlon Brandos (although we *never* forgave him for getting fat) – but there's a kind of condescending 'they're just brawn over brain' attitude which maintains that whilst they may be physically attractive and capable, they're not really *in* with the ecto-supremacists.

Don't you *think*?

Gotcha.

Rules are born of thought. Now I'm not an anarchist, I just believe that rules, unless you make them for yourself from your own sense of inner values, are the bars on the prison of conformity. Remember Osho's first commandment – *"Never obey anyone's command unless it is coming from within you also."*

This is the *power*, the *point*, of the statement nothing is true. Truth is subjective; truth needs to be *your* truth. As I was writing this, somewhere on the planet, the child that would bring the earth's population to seven billion was being born. That's a lot of variables...

Anything is possible, even *telepathy*, if you go deeper than your mind. What's that old chestnut? Eighty-five per cent of communication is non-verbal? Well what's the eighty-five per cent made up of then? We should drop the E off E.S.P. 'cos it ain't extra, it's just sensory perception.

Now I'm not one of those shrinks who suggests that all you have to do is get in touch with your emotions and you'll be sorted – sure, you need to be alive to your feelings but they aren't always reliable, ask anyone who's ever been paranoid. But dig deeper, learn to use the information in your body, in your intuition, in your senses, your perception, your emotions, your intellect, your eyes, your ears, your nose, get the *whole* system firing on all cylinders and you're well on your way to self-remembering.

Here are some tips for training your senses:

Find some kind of meditative practice – that doesn't necessarily mean sitting cross-legged in contemplation, walking is good, so are mundane repetitive tasks like washing-up as already outlined or digging the garden – they calm the mind, get you into your body and balance the whole system.

Practice the self-remembering technique of combining your inner and outer experience.

Look at the back of your hand for ten minutes. Boring, isn't it? Until you push beyond the tedium threshold and see what's always been there but you never noticed because you didn't take the time. We generally only notice our bodies in times of extremes; when did you last pay attention to your kneecap?

When you cracked it on the edge of the coffee table I'll bet. But it's a marvel of engineering, and whether you notice it or not it usually does a magnificent, strenuous and complex job without complaining. Don't wait until the system stops working before you value it.

Go for a walk and listen. Prioritise your ears over your eyes, notice the wind in the trees, the animal sounds and birdsong, traffic, police sirens, the rain falling, the natural opera that is going on around you at all times. Or listen to a song that you've been familiar with for a long time, but this time just listen to the bass drum, listen past the vocals and the forefront sounds, tune your ears so that you can isolate that rhythmic fat thump – it's always there, and if it wasn't you'd notice the gap... Check out the high hat – it only happens four times – on The Stones' *Angie*. It's sublime. Or the way the bass guitar comes in late on the live version of *Midnight Rambler*, Track 1, Side 2, *Get Your Ya Ya's Out*. It's just beautiful. The snare shot intro to Dylan's *Like a Rolling Stone*, or for that matter, the Hammond organ all the way through. Check out your favourite tunes in this way and it's like hearing them for the first time all over again. Oh yeah, I forgot, the twelve-string outro on *Jumpin' Jack Flash*, I've loved that song for over thirty years and I only just noticed it...

Smell – ahhh, one of the most repressed and persecuted of all the senses. Go to Glastonbury and don't wash for a week, smell nature in and on you, let your body have its natural scent and feel your aliveness, your sexiness, and your true animal nature... Just don't fall in the toilets.

As a young man I broke all the rules. In my thirties I broke none. In neither did I connect with myself, with my integrity, with my own sense of ethics, with the reality that *nothing* is *true*, and *everything*... is permitted.

I'd suggest that you make two rulebooks. In the first, list all the rules you inherited, that you learned, that you live with unquestioningly, obediently, unconsciously. Take your time, write them down in full and then – burn them. And as you watch them cremate, know that you're consigning them to the fire, to turn to ash, that they are no longer yours to obey.

Next, get a fresh book (and not some tatty old Ryman's ring-bound piece of crap, get something leather bound and precious) and write a new list of rules, your rules, from your heart, from your truth, from your integrity. No one else ever need see them or approve of them; they're your rules. But you *must* follow them, for as long as they work anyway. The great thing about your rules is you can rewrite the book whenever you feel, and you'll probably need to as you grow and deepen and change.

Below is an example of some of my rules. You'd be forgiven for asking, *'so where were those rules when you were cheating on your wife?'* Fair point. NON EXISTENT. These are rules that I've created on the back of that experience. What's more, they are rules that I aspire to, and rules that I still break. A lot.

It's a journey…

Whatever you do, don't follow them, they're *my* rules. By all means steal some of them if they ring true, but don't follow them because you read them here. And now you're going – *ok, must not follow these rules, they're his rules and he says I mustn't follow them* – shit, I said don't listen to me, look… just check these out and then write your own…

- Be sensitive to others.
- Behave with integrity.
- Behave respectfully.
- Show gratitude.
- Be clear at all times.
- Have and show appreciation for life.
- Be non-judgmental of yourself and others.
- Always seek the truth.
- Be compassionate.
- Never moan.

- Never feel sorry for yourself.
- Be courageous; refuse to follow the impulses of fear.
- Trust that the world is on your side.
- Put your attention on the positive in every situation.
- Honour your needs without having to seek outside approval.
- Have patience with setbacks.
- Harm no one.
- Take responsibility for your actions.
- Experience your shadow in order to go beyond it.
- Know that you are loved.
- And always, always look for the AFGO.

* * *

Nothing is true.

Everything is permitted.

Don't do things in half measures – go all the way.

Live authentically *and* responsibly.

Remember, at all times – *you* wrote this story.

Don't overthink things; develop your intuition by finding your own meditative practice – allow your instinctive self to flourish.

Rewrite the rulebook.

Observe yourself lovingly.

Chapter 5

Think Like a Serial Killer...*

Those who consider the Devil to be a partisan of Evil and angels to be warriors for Good accept the demagogy of the angels. Things are clearly more complicated.
Milan Kundera said that...

Ultimately a hero is a man who would argue with the gods, and so awakens devils to contest his vision. The more a man can achieve, the more he may be certain that the devil will inhabit a part of his creation.
Norman Mailer said that...

The devil made me do it.
Flip Wilson said that...

Sometimes you have to do something unforgivable just to be able to go on living.
Carl Jung said that...

(*Initially I titled this chapter *Behave like a Serial Killer*, but there's legal and humanitarian ramifications with that one...)
An old Cherokee chief was teaching his grandson about life:

"A fight is going on inside me," he said to the boy. *"It is a terrible fight and it is between two wolves – a dark wolf and a light wolf. One is evil – he is anger, envy, sorrow, regret, greed, arrogance, self-pity, guilt, resentment, inferiority, lies, false pride, superiority, self-doubt, and ego. The other is good – he is joy, peace, love, hope, serenity, humility, kindness, benevolence, empathy, generosity, truth, compassion, and faith. This same fight is going on inside you – and inside every other person, too."*

The grandson thought about it for a minute and then asked his grandfather, *"Which wolf will win?"*

The old chief replied, *"the one you feed."*

I was born on the fourth of July.

Big deal – don't mean nuthin' in Slough.

It does, however, mean something in India, and that something is not all that easy to... *digest.*

Whilst studying Tantra in the temples of Tamil Nadu a few years ago, I learned that in Vedic astrology people born on the fourth of the month are aligned with the demon Rahu.

Rahu?

Wikipedia suggests that:

Rahu is a snake that swallows the sun or the moon causing eclipses.

And?

In the East he is considered *"inauspicious."*

Ah...

He signifies cheats, pleasure seekers, drug dealers, outcastes and irreligious people.

Ummm...

Rahu is seen as a demon who does his best to plunge any area of life he controls into chaos, mystery, and cruelty.

And all that for seventy pounds an hour...

There is no equal to Rahu when it comes to giving fame, fortune, prestige and authority, which is probably the reason why Western astrologers regard it as the greatest benefic force.

Not all bad then...

But...

Rahu's characteristics are in some ways similar to those of the Devil.

Shit.

See – despite my early propensity to rule breaking, inside I always thought of myself as good. I was a good person, one of the good guys, an all round good... *egg.*

Wasn't I?

Strange thing is, realising – what I had always suspected – that I am not entirely good... was a huge relief. I mean, being good, doing good, meaning good, playing good was something ... of... a *drag.* A straitjacket. A pain in the arse.

My first *ever* memory, and I'm talking eighteen months old and it's a memory *not* a dream, was of an angel and a demon standing next to my bed. And it was the *demon* that interested me...

As Shakespeare said, *"an overflow of good converts to bad".*

(There'll be a few Catholic priests cringing right now. And policemen, and politicians, and lawyers, and doctors, and *therapists...*)

But then, only Allah is perfect.

You know that one right?

I love that; it saves my obsessive-compulsive ass every time. Every Persian carpet, no matter how exquisite, how sublime, how perfectly woven or hand knotted, no matter how downright *beautiful*, has a deliberate flaw in it. The carpet maker wouldn't *presume* to create something flawless, and that's because?

Only Allah is perfect.
No one is right all the time.
No one is good all the time.
Everyone breaks the rules.

No one is perfect.

Everyone is flawed.

(And I'll tell you what, the 'bad' things I've done? They're the times when I've either had the most fun, or learned the most. Or both.)

I mean, take *'(I Can't Get No) Satisfaction'* right, greatest single pop product in the history of music, no doubt about it yeah? The whole package, the riff, the hook, the lyrics, the attitude, the sound, the length, it's three and a half minutes of testosterone driven imperfection.

Because it's *riddled* with bum notes. Listen to it next time, and I don't just mean the odd bum note, but big, in your face clanging bum notes. It's shot through with them. And every time Keith switches that fuzz box on and off he either misses the beat and comes in too early with a huge fat buzz, or you can hear the pedal clicking on and off, it's just fantastic; it's the imperfections that make it so *beautiful* because they haven't compromised on the energy. They haven't said 'nice take, but let's go again without that loud fart in the middle Keith.' They've said 'no, *that's* the one, that's the vibe.'

No one does that any more, everything's cleaned up, you wouldn't get Michael Bublé singing off key in a million years, he wouldn't know *how* to, that's why he's so fucking dull. But you listen to the Stones, the Who, Hendrix, Led Zep, Iggy, Nirvana – at any moment any of those guys could fall off stage. Literally. That's what makes it exciting, it's unpredictable, it's real, it hasn't had the life sanitised out of it…

I come from violent stock. I know my violence, have embraced my violence, explored my violence, have befriended my violence. My violence is not hidden from me, and in this way, in this *knowing*, in this *relationship*, I make my choices, which by and large are to be non violent (this wavered somewhat on discovering an intruder in my house at 6.30 one morning but there's a time and a place for everything. *"In this case the householder appears to have been the aggressor..."* Well come on, what would you do if you discovered a scab covered HIV positive drug addict out of his gourd on meow-meow with a pocket full of Viagra alone in the bedroom with your naked sleeping girlfriend?)

So, on the whole, I would say I know my violence.

Any of you that ever spent any time around the therapy and self-development world will no doubt have heard a lot about self-love. It was one of the first things I ever heard when I started on this road – you gotta love *yourself* maaaan, you gotta love yourself before you can love another, it's all about love, you gotta heal and love yourself.

Which kind of pissed me off.

I mean I *got it*, intellectually, I *understood* the value of the concept, but at the same time it made my toes curl, partly because I thought it was New Age therapy bullshit but more importantly because it seemed like a club that I simply could not join.

Because I knew inside that I was unlovable.

And this went on for much longer... than I anticipated.

In fact it wasn't until I started looking at the Shadow years down the line that I realised that something had been omitted from the original instruction to love myself.

A key ingredient.

Self-love has to be...

Unconditional.

Ta da!

'Cos up until then it didn't matter how many people told me what a *nice* person I was, inside I knew that if they *knew* who I really was they'd reconsider.

But if you love yourself, you've got to love the whole package right? I don't mean you've got to *like* everything you do; you've just got to *observe* yourself lovingly.

THAT MEANS *ACCEPTING* ALL THAT YOU ARE.

You can't just love yourself for being nice, kind, sensitive and oh so creative. You have to love YOU.

By observing. Lovingly.

Now you might find this challenging, you might really struggle with this suggestion, you might even disagree with me completely, but there's an important thing to consider here if you do.

I'm right.

Sorry.

So anyway, back to the Shadow and here's a tale that illustrates it rather well, a tale that struck me around about the same time that I was getting into *Apocalypse*, from a book of interviews and first-hand accounts from the Vietnam war. There's this one guy in particular whose story stayed with me. He was a regular Middle America middle-class cheerleader-dating football-playing college jock, got drafted aged eighteen, finds himself in 'the Nam', as much weed and smack as he could eat, no rules, no law, no restrictions, officer pisses you off you shoot him in the back next time you go into action... I guess you could say uncontained.

So anyway they give him a big gun, and flying in a helicopter over a village one sunny afternoon he reckons he must have *personally* shot a hundred or more women and children. Said he *knew* they weren't VC, that all the people ran into a river to get away and that he and his buddies hovered over them and wiped them out en masse. Turkey shoot.

So at the end of his tour he rotates back home to his middle-class life in Middle America. Gets married to an ex-cheerleader, has a whoop of kids, becomes the manager of the local hardware store, drinks beer and goes bowling with his middle-class buddies on a Friday night. And you know what he says? He says, *"I'm* normal. *I'm normal, as normal as you can get, and I did... I did that. I killed all those people. And I'm normal."*

What's *not* normal to me is that he's willing to make that

statement, willing to wake up enough to question what he did, not go with the standard *"I was just following orders"* bullshit. He massacred women and children.

He's a regular guy.

He's normal.

'Cos as I've already laboured to explain, this idea of being good is downright dangerous i.e. *good* old Dr. Shipman. I mean for fuck sake, it *happened*, and it *happened* because Shipman didn't *look* like a serial killer. We have this fixed idea in society of what the bad guys look like. In the old days they wore black hats so you could easily identify 'em, but shoot, nowadays they could be… they could be… *you.*

But it's a tough thing to do, embrace your own darkness. And oh how we hate to go there, I mean this is part of our fascination with murderers, rapists, serial killers – THEY *are the evil ones*, and as long as we can gaze upon them in the tabloids then we can distract from our own inner monsters.

But you know what I've noticed every time the press gets their hands on a serial killer? The same quotes over, and over, and over again.

"He was such a lovely neighbour."
"He never caused anyone any trouble."
"Always kept himself to himself."
"He was polite and quiet and always willing to help an old lady down from a tree."

Oh don't we just love to point the finger.

THE FACE OF EVIL!
RIPPER'S MISSION TO KILL!
MONSTER AT LARGE!!!!!
KILLER'S SECRET REIGN OF TERROR!
FREDDIE STARR ATE MY HAMSTER!

'Cos as long as it's out *there*, we don't need to look in *here*.

So here's an exercise, and yup, it'll probably upset a few people, and yes, it could be considered in poor taste, but what the hell, here goes:

Consider the worst crime you ever read about.

Meditate on the most twisted act of evil you ever heard of.

Ponder on the most grotesque and nasty event you can recall from history.

Close your eyes and let yourself really *go* there, imagine there's a projector screen hovering in front of you and visualise with as much clarity as you can the images that come from your own heart of darkness, from the musty dank corners of your own inner labyrinth...

And now let's take it a step further.

Imagine that *you* are the perpetrator of these crimes, you are the bad guy, you are the killer, the rapist, the torturer, the monster...

Difficult isn't it? Revulsion and horror kick in really quick, it's not *me* you say; I couldn't do *that* (the horror and revulsion are what separate you from a real serial killer by the way...)

Push through.

Feel what it is to be the demonised one. If you're still finding it hard, imagine the circumstances in which you could kill. What would it take for you to kill someone? Your children being threatened? Your loved one being raped? Your home being broken into (by a scab covered HIV positive drug addict out of his gourd on meow-meow with a pocket full of Viagra alone in the bedroom with your naked sleeping girlfriend)? Your country being invaded?

Keep going until you find your killer, he or she's in there somewhere. Feel the energy, the power, the sensations, the emotion, the physicality.

Stay there, familiarise yourself with the experience as fully as you can, not just once but often – all relationships take time to build and this one with your darkness is no different. You can try it every time you watch the 'news' or read a paper and hear about something that really shocks you (not that I'd recommend you doing either unless you want to believe that the world is an entirely dark and Satanic realm – the 'news' is what some 'news' editor decides will sell his paper, it's not the whole *story*). Imagine you're in the shoes of the perpetrator, know your demons and make them safe.

Didn't like that exercise? Okay, here's an easier one – before reading any further, stop what you're doing right now, close the curtains, turn off your phone and watch all five seasons of the utterly twisted *Breaking Bad* back to back. Now there's an exploration of the dark side if ever I saw one, a TV series that investigates, at great length, the point at which ordinary people turn to the dark side.

But don't get me wrong. This isn't a handbook for mass murder – in fact it's the opposite. *Know* your killer, your rapist, your own demon and you control it. Hence the nice quiet neighbour thing. Even *they* didn't know what they were capable of – because they didn't know and own their demon. (Brett Easton Ellis did this exercise extremely well when he wrote *American Psycho*, causing global revulsion and outrage whilst having the balls to air his filthiest most soiled and rotten laundry in public and simultaneously penning one of the bravest and most brilliant pieces of prose in modern literature.)

I used to work with perpetrators of domestic violence. A big part of the work was ownership. Guys had sooooooo many reasons, so many explanations as to why it wasn't their responsibility.

"The red mist comes down…"
"I'm a nice guy normally, she just pushes my buttons…"
"It's not the real me, it's like someone else takes over…"

And my personal favourite:

"She bruises easily."

All bullshit. All excuses and ways to distance from their own darkness, to remain forgetful.

For a while, when I was first exploring my violence, I got obsessed with the Great War – go figure... There was something grotesque in the metaphor of that vile maelstrom that helped me connect with the suppressed explosiveness of my own inner world. I spent days walking along faded trench-lines in Northern France, baffled at the emotion that I experienced and it took me many years of therapy to join the dots and recognise that it was my own inner conflict that I was connecting to.

And something I absolutely resonated with was, that by all accounts, it wasn't always your really-up-for-it-macho-gung-ho-let's-have-a-crack-at Fritz-kinda-guy that fought the hardest and the bravest.

It was the quiet, shy, retiring, wouldn't say boo-to-a-goose types that went completely schitz with Fritz.

Siegfried Sassoon is a good example – a gentle, upper-class, gay, poetic, refined and distinguished young man who quickly earned the nickname 'Mad Jack' when he went into action. Completely *crazed* in battle.

If you want to write your own rulebook it helps to know what you're capable of, that way you'll know when you're approaching the edge of what is acceptable to *you*. And next time you go over the top, be it road rage, shouting at the kids, silently wishing cancer on your boss, don't bury it, don't push it to the background and into the shadows, shine some light into those dusty corners, have the balls to know your own demon.

You might just make the world a safer place.

* * *

Feed the light wolf, but remember – only Allah is perfect.

Explore your blind spots, the shadowy corners of your soul –
have some empathy for the devil.

Remember – self-love is unconditional.

Accept all that you are.

Watch all five seasons of Breaking Bad. Now.

Observe yourself lovingly.

Chapter 6

Own Your Inner Keef

The trouble with super heroes is what to do between phone booths.
Ken Kesey said that...

I, I will be king and you, you will be queen though nothing will drive them away, we can be heroes, just for one day.
David Bowie said that...

Hatred is a very underestimated emotion.
Jim Morrison said that...

Everything that we see is a shadow cast by that which we do not see.
Martin Luther King, Jr. said that...

Not... the *greatest* Bowie fan. Which doesn't mean I don't *like* him before you throw this book in the bin in disgust – I like the voice; recognise his iconic status; acknowledge he's written some of the greatest rock'n roll tracks of all time (Ziggy in particular is a hard riff to top); I've bought the albums – I've seen him *live* (Glass Spider Tour in '87 – walked out) but he just somehow, *mostly*, doesn't touch me.

I don't have an inner Bowie.

Which leads me deftly back to the subject of the Shadow and in particular the concept of projection.

Huh?

Okay, it was a bit of a leap.

And yes, at seven in the morning it's early for me too to be heading into this kind of heady clinical territory, I haven't even had a coffee or switched on the sound system and all I've been listening to so far is the sound of Tottenham birdlife and the occasional police siren.

But, let us not be deterred, for the news is, mostly, good.

'In Jungian psychology, the **shadow** may refer to (1) the entirety of the unconscious, or (2) an unconscious aspect of the personality which the conscious ego does not recognise in itself. It may be (in part) one's link to more primitive animal instincts,(3) which are superseded during early childhood by the conscious mind.

According to Jung, the shadow, in being instinctive and irrational, is prone to projection: turning a personal inferiority into a perceived moral deficiency in someone else.

Jung also believed that "in spite of its function as a reservoir for human darkness—or perhaps because of this—the shadow is the seat of creativity."

So let's pick that apart, starting with projection, which isn't as complicated as you might think. Look at it this way:

Who's your hero?

Keith Richards...

What is it about Keith that appeals to you?

He's talented and unconventional and defies authority and lives authentically and... he's not *dead*.

Okay – now repeat the sentence substituting the word *Keith* with *I*.

I am talented, *I* am unconventional, *I* defy authority, *I* do my best to live life authentically and *I*... am not dead.

Ahhhh...

And, as we already began to explore with the whole serial killer thing, the same goes for anyone you hate – love 'em or loathe 'em, they're all just mirroring the parts of you that you learned to ignore or avoid.

Projection – geddit?

Yeah, yeah, I know, I thought this area was gonna be the most boring topic *ever* when I first sat down in class to look at this but man it's one of the most exciting ones yet. Do you get me? I mean, it means that *you*... Yes, YOU – are *Elvis*.

Or Marilyn.

Or Mick.

Or John, Paul, George and/or Ringo!

It means you're Clint Eastwood and Marlon Brando and Cleopatra and Bobby Moore and Audrey Hepburn and JFK and Cat Woman and Neil Armstrong and Benny Hill and the list just goes on and on... *forever*.

Oh, and while I'm dropping the *big one* on you we might as well go the whole hog 'cos of course – wait for it – what this ultimately means is... you ready for this? What this means is that you are:

ROD!

Sorry, that was a typo, I meant –

GOD!

Ah ha!

See *God*... is a projection... of *man*.

Now, I've taken it upon myself to personally investigate this one in order to give weight to this very important point and while my findings are a little *sketchy* I've managed to unearth significant evidence that suggests that the original book of Genesis was written either just before or during the Babylonian exile of the 6th century by a scribe named Ezra who my research would suggest was most likely *dyslexic*.

It's a *hunch*...

So, what *history* has given us in Chapter 1, Verse 27 is *'so God created man in his own image, in the image of God created he him; male and female created he them'*.

Whereas, if my theory is correct, and let's face it, it's not exactly a wild card – the guy can hardly write, his grasp of grammar is appalling – what he (probably) *meant* to write was, '*so man created God in his own image, in the image of him created he God; male and female they created he him*'.

And after the last chapter where, with the help of this book, you realised that you are indeed the next Jeffrey Dahmer I thought I'd better throw you a bone and cheer things up a little, so congratulations – you are divine.

No shit. You really are.

Once you get your head around this you'll find that it's one of the most simple and informative techniques for knowing yourself imaginable.

It's just a beautiful thing. If you want to really *know* your true essence, if that's even possible (and we'll explore that further later in the book) – if you want to see what dwells in your own shadow then just look around at everyone that you love or hate.

And this of course is the basis of all storytelling, be it book, theatre or film. It is through our projection onto and identification with the characters to a greater or lesser extent that grips us. We are *all* Willard/Luke Sky Walker/Dorothy whilst also being Kurtz/Darth Vader/The Wizard of Oz (all the same film by the way – think about it).

For me, personally (and remember, I'm not on the happiness train) the Shadow has been given a bit of a bad rap – even the term, Shadow, is of course, dark and murky. Joseph Campbell, yet again, put it rather well when he said, "*it is by going down into the abyss that we recover the treasures of life. Where you stumble, there lies your treasure.*" 'Cos we tend to throw the baby out with the bathwater, we hide our serial killers but our heroes go too and then we end up getting all pumped up watching shit like Die Hard.

And using that film as an example, why is it we get so excited by, and so invested in the death of a 'bad guy' like Hans Gruber?

Because despite his humble beginnings, RADA taught Alan Rickman to play the part of ourselves we want to kill, terribly, terribly well.

But it's all in there, all in the abyss, the diamonds and the shit, the wonderful, fertile shit. We've already worked with owning our inner Keef, so let's try it again, it's a wonderful exercise and it never fails to set part of me free.

So let's try Adolf.

I fucking hate Nazis. I mean if there was anything that I'd go to war over, it's racism, if there's anything I'd KILL FOR, it's people hating other people because of their race, creed or colour (the more observant of you will note the irony already creeping in here...)

My children are part Ay-rab, my girlfriend Indian.

Which makes me the least racist person I know.

So I'm driving along the M1 after a particularly heavy, deep, spiritual retreat where I'd really cleansed my soul and communed with nature and connected with the great oneness that joins us all and there's this fucking Skoda Fabia ('*the hatchback with class*') going about sixty miles an hour in the fast lane, right? And pretty soon I feel my teeth gritting and I'm definitely NOT two chevrons away and I can see inside that the car is packed with like half a dozen people so the driver can't even see me tailgating in the rear mirror...

Eventually, like two fucking *hours* later, they drift blindly into the middle lane and I'm able to roar past in my pumped up turbo charged sport suspension Subaru Forester, the 2.5-litre DOHC EJ25D four-cylinder boxer engine making 165 hp at 5600 rpm and I can *feel* the automatic transmission sending 90 per cent of the engine's torque to the front wheels and 10 per cent to the rear wheels for better steering control and braking performance using a computer-controlled, continuously variable, multi-plate transfer clutch.

And as I burn past them in a defiant cloud of contempt and

righteous superiority I shoot them a leftward glance that says, 'get the fuck off MY motorway,' and as I do so, I see that the car is full of Muslim women wearing the full Purdah rig.

And I hear myself say:

"Fucking *typical*."

And not only was there the race thing in there, there was the gender thing too.

Both barrels.

And soooooo, I observed myself lovingly and realised that I'm a racist misogynistic *bastard*.

Okay, so it doesn't make me Hitler, but you get the process. The American writer Ken Wilber has a great technique for owning your projected shadow. He says take any statement about any other person and, as with the Keef exercise earlier, substitute *they* for *I*. Try it next time you're in a really heated argument with someone.

So, "*you stupid, arrogant, selfish shit,*" becomes, "*I am a stupid, selfish, arrogant shit.*" In fact, don't wait until you're in an argument, do it now, bring to mind someone you feel hostile towards and see how it fits *you*. And at first you might reject what you find, what nonsense, I'm not *controlling*, they are much worse than me... Well maybe, Hitler was a tad more racist than me, but it's still there in its essence, it's not about proportion.

Hard isn't it?

Wanna try something even harder?

Make a statement about someone you consider to be really amazing – again I know we've already done this with the first Keef exercise, but if we only ever needed to do something once to perfect it we'd all be superheroes.

Which we all are.

But indulge me.

So go on, try it. Here goes:

Jimi Hendrix was the most talented guitar player ever, he was sexy, handsome, warm, charming with a shy sweetness rarely found in a rock star.

Deeeeeep breath...

Okay – I am... shit, er... I am *quite* a good guitar player, I mean not technically but I have a nice feel and a good ear for a tune... er, fuck – you're joking but no, okay, I am sexy, I'm just English and, therefore, probably the first ever Englishman apart from Mick Jagger to consider that I might be, gulp, sexy... to some people.

I used to be handsome, I wish I'd known it at the time and I suppose, again, to *some* people, they might consider me handsome even though I'm going bald and whilst I don't really drink beer I'm beginning to get a bit of a belly and my teeth are fucked and I hide my jowls behind my beard but apart from that, oh, and I've got terrible posture but apart from that I suppose I've got quite a nice mouth and green eyes and my nose isn't too big and I've got good cheek bones so I guess some people might think I'm handsome.

Shit.

This is harder than I remembered.

Warm. Yes, I can get with that. I am warm.

On a good day... When I'm not being cold and distant and withdrawn.

Charming with a shy sweetness oh for fuck sake COME ON...

Enough.

You get the picture, and yes, it surprised me that for most people, owning your monsters is hard, but owning your brilliance is much, *much* harder. I guess it was inevitable that at some point I would get round to quoting from Marianne Williamson's poem *Our Deepest Fear* so let's get it over with:

We ask ourselves
Who am I to be brilliant, gorgeous, talented, fabulous?
Actually, who are you not to be?
You are a child of God.

Sorry.

So, anyway, although this chapter has remained resolutely dark for the most part I still can't stress enough just how cool it is to own this stuff (clinically speaking). It means that wherever you look, you can find yourself, we all have multiple, limitless, ever shifting personalities that make up this thing that we call I, that if you look hard enough you'll realise doesn't even *exist*, it's just this mass of characteristics and adopted behaviours and mannerisms and the best you can ever hope for is to get to know just *some* of this cast of thousands that run riot within our beings.

And that brings me back to Rahu, the demon that I am. The first workshop I ever did was in '92 at the Centre for Transpersonal Psychology. We did a couple of days on what they called sub-personalities, which just means aspects of yourself, and during a deep visualisation exercise I was confronted by this freaky half-snake half-Jesus type figure who accosted me with the warning, *'I'm your creativity, your sexuality and your addictive side all rolled into one. Neglect me – and I'll fuck you up.'*

It made an impression, and I understood the message – it's a daily choice for me, be creative or be destructive, there's not a lot of grey areas, but I can't say that I paid it the attention it deserved.

And so almost twenty years later I was in a three thousand-year-old Shiva temple in some obscure Southern Indian outpost when I happened to look up and there was an ancient, vibrant painting on the ceiling of a half-man half-snake demon.

"This guy on the ceiling?" I asked the guru dude who was my guide. *"I… I've seen him before. Who is he?"*

And the guru dude looked me in the eye and replied:

"He… is you."

And so, another major tattoo later, I'm now paying more attention to Rahu, the demon of eclipses.

But although they're all parts of *us,* the Luke Sky Walker that you see isn't the same one that I see. Sure, there are similarities, but we fill out these archetypal characters with our own flesh and blood. And why do you burst into tears when Lassie finally comes home or Old Yallah gets a cap in his scrawny rabid ass?

That's *your* grief that is.

It's what I call the Princess Di syndrome.

Oh noooo – he's not going to have a go at our Princess Diana? I mean it's bad enough with all this stuff about Satan and serial killers but NOT Diana...

No, I've got nothing against Diana although I can't say I'm from Royalist stock. It ain't *personal.* I'm just intrigued by the phenomenon of what happened when she died. Suddenly... it was okay...

To cry.

And I'll tell you what...

What will you tell us Jerry?

I'll tell you what, most of those people crying about our Di, like mebbe ninety-nine point nine per cent of those people crying about our Di, i.e. like *everyone* apart from her *kids,* weren't actually crying about our Di, it's just it was suddenly open season on bawling your eyes out for ONE WEEK ONLY and so all those unwept tears for yer Nan and yer Mum and yer pet hamster Silver who croaked in 1967 and the boyfriend you split up with when you were fourteen and the tenner you lost on the fuckin' gee-gees last Wednesday came pouring out in a kind of mass hysteria unseen since VJ Day.

And I *know* what you're thinking, you're thinking not only is he a misogynistic racist but he's an anti-royalist insensitive cynic too.

And maybe I am, maybe I am but *come on* – the week before the crash nobody gave a fuck about Princess Diana beyond a bit of gossip and titillation.

There – I said it. Someone had to.

It's not like I was hanging in there for a knighthood anyway.

Moving swiftly on from this dung heap in which I seem to be progressively burying myself, let's return to the safety of Jung and his statement, *"sometimes you have to do something unforgivable just to keep on living"* ringing in our ears, let's return to the earlier Wikipedia quote and the parts we haven't yet unpicked:

- (The Shadow) may be (in part) one's link to more primitive animal instincts, which are superseded during early childhood by the conscious mind.
- Jung believed that "in spite of its function as a reservoir for human darkness—or perhaps because of this—the shadow is the seat of creativity."

Which deserve a chapter apiece...

* * *

Own and use your projections to get to know yourself.

See the greatness hidden in your shadow.

Recognise the story you see as your own.

Observe yourself lovingly.

Chapter 7

Pablo Picasso was Never Called an Asshole

The creative is the place where no one else has ever been. You have to leave the city of your comfort and go into the wilderness of your intuition. What you'll discover will be wonderful. What you'll discover is yourself.
Alan Alda said that...

The chief enemy of creativity is 'good' sense.
Pablo Picasso said that...

Making the simple complicated is commonplace; making the complicated simple, awesomely simple, that's creativity.
Charles Mingus said that...

We are the facilitators of our own creative evolution
Bill Hicks said that...

Okay you cunts, let's see what you can do now.
Hit-Girl said that...

So let's start, arse about face as my Nan used to say, with the second statement:

in spite of its function as a reservoir for human darkness – or perhaps because of this – the shadow is the seat of creativity.

Which is a hell of an intriguing statement.

And one I can get and as we've seen already, our brilliance is hidden in the same dark cupboard as our malevolence.

I mean *creativity*, shit – that's a book in itself. But seeing as we're here, what *is* this thing we call creativity?

And I have to admit that separating this chapter out from the next one which is on sex was a hard one to do 'cos y'know what? I believe they're one and the same, energetically speaking. Which takes us East and to Tantra, and I'm not talking about Westernised sex sells huffin'n a puffin' Sting'n Trudie endorsed Neo-Tantra, I'm talking about the real deal, Indian and Tibetan Tantra, dark, mysterious can't hardly even find it on the Sub-Continent kinda scary Left Hand Path Tantra.

Because the Tantra that I learned about in the formidable temples of Tamil Nadu taught me that *sexuality* is *creativity* is *life-force* – they don't separate. In the West we tend to compartmen-talise ourselves, calling upon our sexuality when we make love, our creativity when we paint a picture. In the east they don't differentiate.

And that's the secret.

I write from my hips, from my pelvis, from my cock.

Oh *yuk*, oh no, really, he's gone *way* too far this time…

But I *do*…

Difficult though it may be – resolutely outta the comfort zone.

That's the zone where creativity lies – on the ledge beyond the edge…

Poor old Prince Charles got into a load of trouble a few years ago when he made some statement about the whole X Factor scene, saying that nowadays everyone believed that they were entitled to their fifteen minutes of fame but that some people just weren't talented.

Okay, gonna put my balls back on the block here but y'know what?

HE'S FUCKING RIGHT.

And I've haven't done an abrupt about turn and gone all pro-monarchy all of a sudden and I'm not even referring to the talent comment – most people have some kind of gift or latent ability at least – what I'm agreeing with is the entitlement, the idea that it isn't hard.

You imagine it's easy being a Spice Girl? And yeah – I'm old enough for the Spice Girls to come to mind when I think of a pre-fab band, hell, I used to watch The Monkeys when they were first broadcast, and I'm still hip enough to have never heard anything by One Direction. Shit, I'm so hip I just had to Google them to make sure they *exist…*

Anyway, back to the Spices bless 'em. Whatever you believe, they worked hard, indeed the very fact that they really weren't the most talented… I'm hesitating here – what were they? Singers? No. Actors? Maybe. Whatever, the very fact they weren't the most talented *people* – yeah, that's the word I was looking for, people – in the world (you ever seen the *audition tapes?)* made them work extra hard and they earned it. Same with The Stones, you read Andrew Loog Oldham's book *'Stoned'* and you'll hear tape ops and engineers from about '62 going, *'doesn't matter about their reputation as bad boys, that came later, in the beginning they were the most professional, hungry, completely on top of their game kids you ever met'.*

Creativity is hard work, as the writer and poet Dorothy Parker summed up when she said, *"I hate writing – I love having written."* It's a bastard, but if all it took was hard work those of us that bothered to apply ourselves would all be best-selling novelists and multi-millionaire artists. No, it's that mystical ingredient that somehow comes from the reservoir of human darkness that makes it so elusive.

One of the tricks I've found – and I'm employing it *right now* – is the willingness to be shite. Right now I am writing utter shit. Garbage. I'm basking in my own permission to be as far from brilliant as possible, 'cos to attempt to create a great piece of work is the shortest route to mediocrity that I know.

You imagine kids worry about how good their painting technique is? No way, children's paintings are rubbish man, they're the worst artists in the world, they can't draw for toffee, their notion of composition, focal point and perspective is tenuous at best (don't even start me on their *appalling* grasp of grammar and narrative structure when it comes to writing about what they did in the summer holidays). And what do they believe? They believe they're amazing.

And they are.

We take these crap paintings and pictures that look absolutely *nothing* like a car/house/fairy/flower and we exhibit them all over the walls of our houses. And we tell them they're good.

And children...

Are prolific.

Go figure.

I remember talking with radio broadcaster Sean Rowley years ago and he made me aware of a really important detail – what I call the glimmer in the darkness. He said:

> *I can't remember my dad ever giving me any kind of encouragement on anything, but I remember my uncle walking into my bedroom, I can remember where I was sitting, where the desk was, what I was wearing, every detail, and he said to me, 'remember Sean, you can do anything you set your mind to.' I fucking remember that... like some magical spell being passed down.*

This is now a man who's living his dream of playing music for a living because of one encouraging comment in an otherwise barren wasteland.

I don't know if it's just me, but I find that really touching. And there's a pattern there that I see – it just takes one person to shine a light on a kid, and no matter how much darkness there's been it's like a beacon that guides people through. I don't know if there's anyone who's been through my practice room that hasn't had a glimpse of that; for me it was my Grandparents.

But it's a conundrum isn't it – once you've got the experience, as Picasso and so many other artists discovered, how do you unlearn? How to become innocent again? I don't know the answer – maybe keep taking risks, stay away from the comfort zone, do things you've never tried – I've never written a self-help book before. Maybe I still haven't…

Children are by nature naïve and creativity is one of many areas where experience isn't necessarily a bonus. I read this amazing fact in a book about D Day (yeah I know, there's a lot of war books being referenced here, I'm a guy okay?) Anyway, on D Day the Americans had like *thousands* and thousands of veterans who'd fought through North Africa and Sicily and Italy. Really experienced soldiers, battle-hardened, guys who knew what it was to go to war.

D'you know how many of them they put on the first wave of boats going into Omaha Beach?

Not one.

Nope.

'Cos they recognised that if they put these soldiers in the first wave the minute they hit the beach they'd go, *'you gotta be kidding me man? I mean, there's like – no fucking way I'm getting off this boat, these odds are too much…'*

And so, the clever people back at mission control put all the kids fresh out of boot camp in the first wave, they ran out of the boats and got mown down in their thousands but you see… they didn't *know* that those beaches were impregnable. They didn't have the *experience* that told them that it was impossible to breach the Atlantic Wall, that men against barbed wire and machine guns just didn't make *sense*, so they just kept on going and *that*… is why we don't speak German in England today.

Ignorance is not only bliss; it's *essential* sometimes if you want to achieve greatness. Hence the difficult second album syndrome – you *know* just what it took to produce the first one by then. Shit, I'm approaching fifty and I wouldn't do a third of what I achieved when I was younger with what I know now, there's no way, I'd be thinking 'na, that just doesn't add up, I'm gonna go bankrupt/ look a fool/be embarrassed/fail miserably if I try that.

Have a look back – what do you consider to be your achieve-ments – being able to recognise that might in itself is one of them, I've never met anyone who considers themselves successful, success seems to always be conceptualised as a future event – when I'm rich, when I've done this, that or the other, when I've met the person of my dreams.

See what you can come up with – for me it's playing to a full house for three consecutive years at the Edinburgh Fringe with the theatre company I founded when I was eighteen. I look back at that and think – 'how the fuck did I manage that? What was I *thinking*?' But how to take the essence of that naïve eighteen-year-old and apply it to *this*, whatever this is? For me, in the writing of this book, it's been not to plan, to not *think*, to not puzzle it all out, to not consider the risks, to be wilfully ignorant and see where the ride takes me.

Osho said, *"if there is no chaos, there is no creativity,"* which is an interesting way to look at it. You gotta get messy, you gotta get covered in paint, but perhaps darkest of all, you gotta face your own demons because there's no greater food for your self-loathing and doubt than your creative offerings – it's where we stand truly naked before the world and say, *'look, this is of me, it's of my essence, it's of my soul'* – unless you're faking it of course. And this is what makes so many of us shy away from bringing forth our creativity, for better or worse, those inner voices – and I can hear them now as I write – that say, *'who are you to believe that you're any good? What makes you so special – you know you're going to be ridiculed and found out don't you? You know that people will laugh and sneer at your pathetic attempts?'*

There's not a person alive that doesn't know that script in some shape or form, and all I can say is, sorry – it ain't going away.

Huh?

Isn't this book supposed to help me grow beyond my limitations, what does he mean it ain't going away? And why's he saying ain't instead of isn't, I thought he was public school educated?

It's not going away because it's part of you, it's what Freud defined as the super-ego and Fritz Perls, godfather of Gestalt therapy, defined as the top-dog. I'd simplify it and just call it the self-critic.

But whatever name you give it, it's yours to keep. For all the effort you make to get rid of it you might as well try and unlearn that the sky is blue or two plus two equals four. See, humans are incredible sponges of learning, I mean, by the time we're five we're usually fluent in a language, we've learned how to walk, feed and dress ourselves, how to count and draw rudimentary shapes, and that's just the beginning. The trouble is – we don't have much of a filtration system. So, you teach a kid two plus two, not to take sweets from strangers, to look left and right when they cross the road; that big boys don't cry and if you aren't sweet and pretty you're a nasty little girl and it all goes in with the same innocent willingness to learn.

And by the time you're an adult you've been bombarded with a million different negative messages that have been taken in and become part of the monster that is your self-critic. Every negative shaming message from your parents, teachers, school bullies, adverts and manipulative magazine covers, comes at us from all angles and never stops nurturing the beast which gets hungrier the more it's fed, the bigger it grows the more presence and influence it has.

And these messages don't even have to be deliberate; in fact the covert ones are often the hardest to spot. I remember clocking this in a conversation with my mum when I told her I was planning to train to be a psychotherapist.

"That's a nice idea," she said. *"And why don't you do something else at the same time like an evening class in plumbing – so that you've got something to fall back on if it doesn't work out."*

Now there is *no* doubt in my mind whatsoever that her intentions were good, supportive even. But of course that's not how it landed in my twisted psyche. Roughly translated it went, *"you useless piece of shit, who do you imagine you are attempting something as complex as psychotherapy, you don't have two brain cells worth rubbing together, stick to something menial and within your grasp like ramming your arm down other people's u-bends."* (No disrespect intended to tradespeople who specialise in installing and maintaining systems used for drinking water, sewage, and drainage).

Those covert ones get in under the radar.

But having doomed you by saying it's never going away I don't mean you have to resign yourself to your own internal tyranny. That film *A Beautiful Mind* starring Russell Crowe illustrates what I would suggest is the best treatment plan.

Now forgive me if I get some of the details wrong, I didn't care much for the movie and it doesn't really matter anyway, I'm just making a point. From what I remember Crowe plays some clever bastard rocket scientist or something and at the beginning of the film there are various characters who he interacts with that give him somewhat shitty advice, like drown the baby in the bath'n stuff.

As the film progresses it becomes apparent to us, the viewer, that these characters are delusional figures visible only to Crowe who's got some kind of bonkers mentalist condition. Ultimately there's a point where he recognises that these figures aren't real and he has a conversation where in effect he says, *'you've been with me all my life, in fact I've often trusted you as friends, but from now on I'm just going to ignore you.'*

For the rest of the film the same characters are present, but Crowe no longer interacts with them and they sit quietly by without influence or effect.

You see where I'm going right?

In the early days when I was less experienced I used to fight them, and when I became a therapist that's what I used to say to people – imagine taking your self-critic out to the woods, get it to dig its own grave and blow its brains out. I was watching a lot of Scorsese at that time. I used to get them to beat the shit out of cushions with baseball bats and scream and shout at their super-ego, but then I realised there's nothing more a top-dog likes than a real good fight. You say, *"fuck off"* and it says, *"you gonna make me bitch?"* You say, *"I'm NOT stupid,"* and it's gonna come back with, *"who you trying to kid you fucking moron?"*

It's like pouring petrol on a fire.

No, the best defence is to ignore, to catch the attack for what it is – which takes Jedi level skill in itself – and simply ignore it. To observe yourself lovingly, recognise the assault, and turn away unaffected.

Your self-critic is the greatest enemy of creativity; your self-compassion – its guardian angel.

How else are you going to find your flow, your rhythm, your voice, how else are you going to push through the thick membrane of self-doubt to get into the zone?

Self-compassion and consciousness is the answer – you have to be gentle enough with yourself not to be swamped by the demons and curious enough to see the hurdles without falling.

The first thing that usually occurs when people sit down to be creative is that the distractions kick in – the urge to check your Facebook page, to make another coffee, light another cigarette, check your emails and log onto YouPorn. I say *do* it, indulge the little fuckers – similar to your self-critic, to resist is to give them energy – wear the bastards out and you'll find that after not too long the desire to create becomes a yearning and the distractions fall away like scales from a dead fish.

When I first started writing years ago I did it with the belief that I *should* do it for eight hours a day. The word *should*, by the way, is a pretty good indicator that your self-critic is loose. I'd read somewhere that Steven King wrote from six in the morning 'til eight at night and so I figured *that* was the way. The self-critic thrives on rules.

But then I picked up a colour supplement that had a piece on a day in the life of various well-known authors. I forget who any of them actually were, but it's not important, what really hit me was how one of them described their working day.

He worked out of his garden shed, in which he had a laptop, a PlayStation and an electric guitar. He said that he spent about twenty minutes writing; then he'd move onto the PlayStation and then the guitar and then back to writing again. He said he couldn't possibly write for more than twenty minutes at a time.

It blew my mind. It broke the rules – rules that I'd invented, rules that didn't exist. Because, when it comes to creativity...

Nothing is true.

Everything is permitted.

Even PlayStation.

This was also true of my therapy practice, and I guess you could apply the principle to almost any situation you might be unhappy in. I'm dead lucky in that I work with some truly inspirational people. But it wasn't always that way and it wasn't about luck – it's careful selection based on chemistry. I learned a long time ago who I could and couldn't work with based simply on whether I felt a connection or not. Now, whilst that might sound a little too much in the spirit of ethnic cleansing the bottom line is that for some people I'm the best person in the world to work with, for others the worst – shit, you could go see Freud but if you thought he was an asshole it probably wouldn't do you or him any good. Like any relationship, chemistry is the most important part of it.

In the beginning, for the first four or five years, I worked with anyone and everyone because I had a 'rule' in my head that as a psychotherapist it was my duty to be available to anyone who walked through the door.

And because I'd worked in prisons and run groups for violent offenders I tended to get the people who my colleagues took one look at and went, *'no way – send him to Mr.Hyde...'*

And very quickly I became burned out and began to feel that this really wasn't the job for me, and to be honest my practice wasn't really working 'cos I just didn't want people to come and see me.

Until one day a young actor came in. We had a blast, I totally got where he was at, and I don't know about him but it changed my life. At the end of the session after he left I remember reflecting, *'why can't all my clients be like that?'*

And this little light went on.

'Ahhhhhhh…'

I started putting the word around that I was a therapist who specialised in working with people in the arts and my practice took off like never before and I've never looked back.

As Joseph Campbell used to say – I was *in flow*, I was following my bliss.

You just have to find your own rhythm and then everything will flow. While I've been writing this I've watched three-quarters of Kick-Ass 2 – shit by the way – eaten a bowl of pasta, checked all my incoming emails, commented on a few posts on Facebook and window shopped on eBay. Porn's not my thing but if it was you can guarantee I'd have been there by now. Each time the writing becomes a strain I'll go and play for a while until the urge to write grows to a point that's irresistible.

Your rhythm will be completely different, you'll have to experiment but once you find it…

There'll be no stopping you.

I'm going to finish that movie now and then we can have an awkward chat about sex.

* * *

Sexuality is creativity is sexuality – no difference.

Be willing to be shit in order to be brilliant.

Look at your life and see if you can find the source of the glimmer in the darkness.

Value your innocence – remember there is a cost to becoming an 'expert'.

Recognise your self-critic for what it is and send it into exile.

Self-compassion is the guardian angel of creativity.

Follow your bliss.

Observe yourself lovingly.

Chapter 8

I'd Love to Spill the Beans with You All Night

Sex is full of lies. The body tries to tell the truth. But, it's usually too battered with rules to be heard, and bound with pretences so it can hardly move. We cripple ourselves with lies.
Jim Morrison said that…

You can't fake creativity, competence, or sexual arousal.
Doug Coupland said that…

Why should we take advice on sex from the pope? If he knows anything about it, he shouldn't.
George Bernard Shaw said that…

I would rather have a cup of tea than sex.
Boy George said that…

I know nothing about sex, because I was always married.
Zsa Zsa Gabor said that…

'Ere – d'you know that forty-one per cent of Cosmopolitan readers reckon they have sex two to three times a week?

I read it on the Internet so it must be true.

You fucking…

Fucking…

Liars.

Of course I could be completely skewed in my data, it being an occupational hazard that I only mix with people who by and large report having shit sex lives given that they're in therapy with *me* and the reality is that the rest of you are at it like steam hammers two, or even three, times a week.

It could be true.

But I very much doubt it.

I just have this hunch that, in Britain anyway, no one knows the real picture because very few people, and this perhaps applies even more so to men, ever go down the pub and go, *'guess what? I haven't had sex in six months'*. I don't imagine people do that.

Oh, and just in case I'm right... sorry. Sorry for being the one to kill the dream. Not that it matters terribly if you're *not* having sex – if that's okay with you – what matters is that you're having the sex that *you* want, as often as *you* want, in the way that *you* want, with the vibrancy, excitation and aliveness that *you* want with someone that *you* want and who wants *you*. It's *you* that's the operative word, not what's NORMAL.

Normal... That amorphous thing that – though everyone who ever talked to me about sex wanted to know what it was – doesn't *exist*.

Repeat after me:

THERE IS NO NORMAL, THERE IS NO NORMAL, THERE IS NO NORMAL a thousand times, or until it begins to implant in your consciousness. And never forget that the notion of normal is just a tool designed to make you feel bad and scared.

The glossy magazines aren't *entirely* driven by ethics you see? Your best interests are not *always* at the centre of what motivates them, what they actually want is to establish and maintain a *notion* of normal, make sure that you feel that you don't fit in – and given that we've established long ago that you're most likely a Gonzo seeker you almost certainly won't – and scare the shit out of you with front line banners like:

IT'S FINALLY HERE! THE DEFINITIVE LIST!

(*Finally*? Really? Like – you're honestly suggesting that we've been waiting for this shit? Ah, you see I'm sorry but... once *again* you've mistaken me for one of those people who gives a fuck).

...THE TEN BEST WAYS TO EXCITE YOUR LOVER IN BED!

By which they really mean:

IF YOU DON'T BUY THIS IRRELEVENT AND USELESS PIECE OF LAZILY CONSTRUCTED HALF THOUGHT OUT DOG SHIT YOU'LL NEVER LEARN THE SECRET OF AROUSING YOUR LOVER MEANING THAT YOUR FEARS THAT YOU'RE UTTERLY HOPELESS IN BED WILL BE CONFIRMED, HE OR SHE WILL ABANDON YOU AND YOU'LL BE LEFT ALONE AND UNWANTED –
FOREVER!

Now, I don't actually believe in the Devil, but if he *does* exist you can bet your life he's got the editor of Hello! (why the exclamation mark?) on some kind of seven-year deal.

The Devil hardly gets a look-in in the Old Testament, although they certainly had well-developed ideas of right and wrong back then, but the whole duality thing really took on a whole new head of steam with the emergence of Christianity. And I'm using Christianity here as a kind of representative for all organised religion, I know less about the others, although Judaism and Islam in particular seem to have... *opinions* on quite a few areas, especially those that I personally would put under the bracket of *fun*.

The thing is, whatever your leaning, we've all been raised in the slipstream of these belief systems. Whilst I have nothing against religion, in fact I observe people with some kind of faith doing better in a crisis than those who don't, what I *do* have a problem with is how it's been used. Which is much the same way glossy magazines are used today within the new religion of celebrity – to control and extort by creating a culture of confusion and fear.

So, who's the scariest figure ever? Dracula? Freddie Kruger? Hannibal Lecter?

Na – straight in at number one: Satan, Lucifer, Beelzebub, Old Nick, Spring Heeled Jack, Mr Scratch, Mephistopheles, the Prince of Darkness, His Satanic Majesty… The Devil.

And why's the Devil so important to organised religion?

Because he's scary.

Why is *that* important?

Because if you want to control people the best way is to make them fearful.

So how does that work?

Tell them, unless they follow your rather blurry dogma that keeps them not only terrified but also never quite sure if they're getting it right or not, that they'll go to hell. Reinforce this by perpetrating hideous acts of genocide, torture, barbarism and war in the name of your god.

And perhaps most important of all, threaten them that if they partake of the most beautiful, divine, pleasurable, god given, delicious, healthy and natural act of creation, the act of sex, that they should feel shame, disgust, self-loathing and guilt of off the scale proportions.

It's reminiscent of Bill Hicks' observation about drug policy. Tobacco and alcohol, two drugs which are legal and *taxable*, make you stupid – they dumb you down. Naturally occurring plants like marijuana and psilocybin mushrooms that *expand* your consciousness are prohibited. Someone up there doesn't want you to be asking too many enlightened questions.

They'd rather you didn't wake up.

Likewise, the church realised a long time ago that if people go around fucking… they feel happier.

Which is counter to the whole 'control the mob' plan. They need people to be unhappy, to suffer, to feel bad and, therefore, need a saviour to lift them from their miserable existence.

And it's worth mentioning here that the Devil was merely an adaptation by the Christian Church of the original pagan horny goat, God of Fuck – Pan.

The tyranny of fear, of right and wrong, good and bad, light and dark, Jesus and the Devil, The Beatles and The Stones, hangs heavy on all our shoulders, it makes it almost impossible to break out and live an authentic, honest existence of aliveness. And in our attempts to deal with the angels and demons that constantly plague our thoughts we retreat to our heads and become alienated from our bodies. As Hamlet said, 'there is nothing either good or bad, but thinking makes it so.'

Sex. Shit, we can't even *talk* about it.

And even I'm hitting a wall here, there's so much to say but how and where to start? When we're up against thousands of years of programming, of indoctrination, of shame.

And where there's shame there's judgement and where there's judgement there's no self-compassion and without self-compassion there is no chance of self-remembering and without that, no enlightenment.

So we really need to deal with this sex thing.

Of course shame takes us back to the fear of exile – we'd rather forget ourselves, be dead inside, dried up husks devoid of creative juices, than risk shame.

Because expression of our sexual desires, even more than expression of our creativity, is probably *the* most vulnerable place any of us go, it's beyond naked, the stakes are so high, and the wounds so deep once cut.

"You want to do *what*?"

Even the tone of voice is enough to do irreparable damage and create an '*I'm not going back there again, fuck that, I'll stick to an occasional missionary position preferably when drunk*' attitude.

That's why sex with strangers is so appealing to many and explains the boom of fuck buddy websites and Grinder apps – the risk of humiliation is greater with... drumroll... someone you *love*.

We're fucked aren't we? Or not?

And so, really chapters on sex and creativity have to also be chapters on vulnerability, shame and the fear of humiliation. Not very sexy I know but go get the *Joy of Sex* if you're looking for tips. The great shame researcher Brené Brown, in her book *Daring Greatly: How the Courage to Be Vulnerable Transforms the Way We Live, Love, Parent, and Lead* says that without vulnerability there is no intimacy.

Interesting point.

Then again in *Mating in Captivity* the Belgian born sex therapist Esther Perel makes the bold statement that it's actually the mass marketing of intimacy by the therapy world and the insistence on total self-disclosure in our relationships that explains why so few people are having sex. She suggests that it's actually mystery and a degree of separateness that creates the sexual spark.

Of course trust is the real issue, the trust to risk showing yourself, and I don't just mean sexually, I mean baring your soul, but also knowing where to hold back. The difference between privacy and secrecy is shame. Privacy feels clean, but secrecy is always accompanied by fear – what would people do if they only *knew*, is our fearful inner script. I mean *shit* – we were talking about inner critics with regard to *creativity* but that's nothing compared to what those demons do with *sex*.

And so rather than deal with sex in an open, honest and courageous way, most of us spend our lives running from those demons in response to bullshit 'rules' that we've innocently ingested as children without awareness or question.

I remember running a sexuality group once and this guy came in and told a story that broke my heart. He said he'd been at the Tate Gallery and he'd seen *the* most exquisite woman. She was young and sweet and radiant and fresh and glowing with a quality of beauty that he said, *"age would never taint, she had the kind of beauty that was eternal."*

"Whoa man – so... so what did you do?" I gasped.

"Do? Well... nothing of course."

"What? What do you mean nothing? What – you didn't tell her?"

"No way, she might have been really offended or laughed at me or hit me or something."

And I feel, shit – is that where we're at? Is that where we've evolved to? I mean, what he felt wasn't predatory, it wasn't lecherous, it was *Shakespearian*... if some stranger came up to me and said something like that I'd remember it forever. But we've all done it; we've all swerved the opportunity to make the world a more beautiful place by sharing our response to beauty.

When I was at school I was the typical uncool, four-eyed spotty kid with a greasy centre parting. But by the time I was in my early twenties things had changed – I had the New York motorcycle cop leather jacket, the drainpipe jeans, the quiff, the shades and I'd learned to smoke without taking the cigarette out of the corner of my mouth.

And so attired one bright spring morning sauntering down Berwick Street in Soho I spied not one, but *three* of the hottest girls ever from my school, girls *so* desperately hot that they had never once glanced in my direction. But now I was cool, now was my chance to saunter across the road and say, *"hi hot chicks – I know you were always too busy snogging the rugby jocks to ever notice me but I'm cool now, I've got the jacket and everything and I always wanted to talk to you but I was too shy and spotty back then but now fate has thrown us together like this maybe we could go get a coffee and stuff?"*

And then who knows, next thing we might have all been back at my squat re-enacting that scene from Clockwork Orange (the one where he has sex with the two girls – not the murder or rape stuff).

So, did I cross the road?

Nope.

No, I went, *'fuck it – they always ignored me, now's my turn.'*

And I *know* what you're thinking, you're thinking maybe I would have been better served paying heed to American clergyman Douglas Horton's cautious words, *'while seeking revenge, dig two graves – one for yourself.'*

But I didn't, my mind was unsullied by such wisdom, and so I stuck my nose up in the air and – making sure they'd seen me – strode off in the other direction.

Which is *why* I didn't see the MOUNTAIN of Great Dane shit that lay piled and steaming in my path, which is *why* I actually tore a muscle in my groin when my blue suede creeper hit the dung at full extension forcing me to execute an impromptu yet near flawless grands ronds de jambs as the crepe sole lost all traction. Eyes on stalks, arms windmilling uselessly I skidded out of control on one foot like a dirty figure skater until somehow I managed to regain control, and jaw set in a determined *that never happened* grimace, I disappeared shamefaced into the fruit and veg stalls of Soho…

The moral to this story? There *is* no moral to this story, unless it's performing spontaneous ballet manoeuvres in blue suede shoes and shit doesn't impress… anyone. Or maybe it's love is not cool. I *hate* all those rules – treat 'em mean, keep 'em keen etc. Like we've all got to pretend we don't give a shit or we're gonna look… What? Weak? Can you imagine if Shakespeare had adopted those cool rules?

> This bud of love, by summer's ripening breath,
> May prove a beauteous flower when next we meet.
> 'Tho that'll never happen, 'cos I'm not gonna call,
> Lest my mates take the piss, by text or by tweet.

So anyway, let's move away from tales of my youthful humiliation and get back to sex. As I was saying – if it's tips you're after, read *The Joy of Sex,* or better still, read *The Guide to Getting It On! A Fun and Mostly Wonderful Book about Sex* by Paul Joannides, which really is the best sex book I've ever read.

And not only does it do what it says on the can but it's the *only* sex manual I ever read which approaches the incredibly dangerous area of sexual feelings towards children.

And makes the extremely brave statement that it's not unusual.

Sharp intake of breath… and relax.

It says it's not *unusual* to have feelings of a sexual nature towards children; IT'S WHAT YOU DO WITH THOSE FEELINGS THAT COUNTS.

Doh.

And there is *such* wisdom in that statement – in giving people permission to have their feelings without imagining, '*oh shit, that makes me a paedophile*' it makes it less likely that those feelings will be buried in some deep dark corner and be allowed to fester and grow.

A client of mine – a man in his late twenties – told me recently that at school the bullies had called him a paedophile. Shit, all we had to deal with when I was a kid was *poof*. The word paedophile hadn't filtered through the media into our consciousness back then, it hadn't yet been used to sell 'news' papers.

My mum grew up in the 1930s in a part of the Chilterns where my family have lived for the last seven hundred years or so. She told me that in the village was the blacksmith, the post office, two pubs, the grocery shop and the child molester. And everyone knew which was which and everyone more or less got on with their lives.

You just avoided the old bloke who interfered with children.

But it wasn't yet harnessed by the press to sell papers which means it wasn't driven underground which means that people talked about it which means that the children were safe.

How did we get from creativity to sex to child abuse?

Through not talking, through repression, through duality – through *right and wrong* – right and wrong, one of the greatest hurdles to self-remembering, the place where it is IMPOSSIBLE to harm anyone or anything. I mean it ain't fuckin' rocket science to figure out why so many Catholic priests, so-called spiritual figure heads and pillars of virtue in a religion laden with guilt and the notion of sex as the original sin, have molested children is it?

And just in case I haven't alienated you all with my contentious opinions, let me throw another in for good measure.

TV presenter, media personality and charity fundraiser, Sir James Wilson Vincent Savile, OBE, KCSG, is the best thing to ever happen in the UK when it comes to sexual abuse.

Because since the story broke of his activities as perhaps the UK's most prolific sex offender, in eighteen years of supporting victims of sexual abuse I've *never* had so many people open up to what happened to them, I've *never* witnessed such courage, I've *never* seen such progress and so many demons slain.

Enough.

We'd heal a lot of things if we could talk more, and we'd have much more fun.

I recently got a Facebook status update from a well-known English actor that said, *'just had a wank'* (which received fifty-six *likes* and fifty-four *comments*, quite impressive statistics I feel you'll agree). Now that, to my mind, makes him a great sexual role model. Because he's simply being honest. About something that… we all do.

Even…

Your mum.

Yes your mum and your dad both have cum faces and they both have had a wank at some time or other as well as full-blown, perhaps even quite experimental, sex – and probably more than just the one time it took to conceive you.

DEAL WITH IT!

I'm so sorry, I keep trying to lighten this chapter up but it just keeps getting so dark. Is it me or is it our culture? I guess the answer is both, sex has been stolen from us, locked away in deep vaults of shame, covered in blankets of guilt, used as a means of control and to sell products from cars to vacuum cleaners to... just about everything. I'm genuinely worried that we've ruined it forever, it's so precious, so delicate, we've gone running around with these massive fuckin' great boots for so long I don't know if we'll ever recover.

We made something so, *so* precious...

Dirty.

The erotic carvings of the medieval Khajuraho temples in India depict:

> *twisting, broad-hipped and high breasted nymphs display their generously contoured and bejewelled bodies on exquisitely worked exterior wall panels. These fleshy apsaras run riot across the surface of the stone, putting on make-up, washing their hair, playing games, dancing, and endlessly knotting and unknotting their girdles.... Beside the heavenly nymphs are extravagantly interlocked maithunas, or lovemaking couples.*

The society of the time believed in dealing frankly and openly with all aspects of life, including sex. The Chandela kings who commissioned the temples were greatly influenced by the Tantric school of thought in which sex is seen as an important part of the path to *enlightenment*.

Hmmmm...

Almost a thousand years earlier:

> *Erotic art in Pompeii and Herculaneum was discovered after extensive excavations began in the 18th century. The city was found to be full of erotic art and frescoes, symbols, and inscriptions*

regarded by its excavators as pornographic. Even many recovered household items had a sexual theme. The ubiquity of such imagery and items indicates that the sexual mores of the ancient Roman culture of the time were much more liberal than most present-day cultures, although much of what might seem to us to be erotic imagery (e.g. oversized phalluses) could arguably be fertility-imagery. This clash of cultures led to an unknown number of discoveries being hidden away again. For example, a wall fresco which depicted Priapus, the ancient god of sex and fertility, with his extremely enlarged penis, was covered with plaster and only rediscovered in 1998 due to rainfall.

They covered an ancient fresco in *plaster*. They *covered it up*. Does that shock you as much as it does me?

In Roman times, what we deem pornographic was considered...

Wallpaper.

See, when you make something shameful, you make people secretive and furtive, you plaster over our sexuality and you drive what I would contest is the most powerful energy on the planet deep underground.

We've sexualised the shit out of everything and yet we can't actually talk about it.

I dare you. I *double dare* you – go and talk to a close friend about sex. I don't mean about your conquests, I mean talk about what it's really *like*, the highs and lows, the pleasure and the disappointment, the satisfaction and the despair.

Can you?

And even if you say yes, I *do* talk like that with my friends, 'cos I know you're out there (and I'll bet good money if you do you're female), can you do it easily? Honestly? In all areas? Are you holding back?

Tell the truth now.

And don't get me wrong, I absolutely believe in privacy, but there's a big difference between privacy and secrecy. Secrecy always has shame attached to it, privacy feels clean, and that's the litmus test. Try it – what feels secretive and shameful? What feels clean and yours to keep.

It's an important distinction.

A chapter on sex was never going to be definitive, in fact it was never going to be much more than a cry for help – we're probably centuries away from ever healing that can of worms. But rather than bum you out totally with, let's face it, what's been a somewhat downbeat chapter, let's try, once again, to end on something more positive.

A good sex life is down to one thing and one thing alone.

And no – it's not how many people you've fucked. Or how often. Or for how long, or in whatever position.

It's down to you having a great relationship with…

Yourself.

Yes, sorry – back to YOU again.

Knowing who you are, what turns you on and off, when, where and how and how not and all the million ever changing variables in between and, here's the important bit, being able to communicate that with clarity, confidence and without shame.

Now that's sexy.

I asked a woman recently if she knew that she was sexy. NO was the reply. And so I set her a homework, which you might want to try. It goes like this:

Go home, spend some time alone in your room, and allow yourself to feel sexy (that's sexy, not sexual – they're not the same although one might follow the other). Allow yourself to feel sexy. Walk around; see where you feel it in your body, notice how you hold yourself.

And now – stop.

Notice the difference when you shut it down, notice *how* you shut it down, what you have to do.

Now turn it up halfway. Notice again what you have to do.

Imagine a volume control, take it up to eight, now down to four, then down half a notch more, now all the way up to ten, now down to two, to one, and now all the way up to eleven!

Being sexy is not something that happens, it's something that you do. It's a decision. Once you become aware of that then you have more control, more self-awareness, and being conscious of your sexiness is an essential ingredient in becoming a satisfied sexual being.

Another great exercise is masturbating; or perhaps a better term if we're going to move away from a word that sounds almost medical, self-pleasuring. I did it recently in a room with fifty people and that was a bit of a *stretch*, but I got the point, to de-mystify and give permission to something that tends to be furtive and loaded with shame. A real challenge can be to do it without fantasy or visual stimulus – a great way to deepen your relationship to yourself. A lot of people – especially men I'm afraid – will respond to this suggestion with horror. *Without porn or fantasy? Are you serious?*

Yes I am.

Try it. Pleasure yourself with nothing but the physical sensations of your own stimulus. Notice what you like, the sensations, the change in your breathing patterns, how quickly or slowly you become aroused, where you experience that arousal (oh, and I'm not talking about a two-minute wank here – take some time, have a bath, set the place up like you might if you were feeling romantic or seductive – I'm assuming you're not on public transport whilst trying this exercise – light some candles, burn some incense, STOP CRINGING).

Take yourself to the brink of orgasm and stop. See what it's like to stop, to let your passion settle a little, to back off, and now start again and take yourself to a place where you can just stay there and enjoy the pleasure without coming or getting bored, and hang there a while. Then if you feel like it, allow yourself to climax, feel the peak as deeply and fully as possible, notice your body sensations, the afterglow as you return to a non-aroused state.

Self-pleasuring – is an art.

It's the simplest trick I know and it's free and it's fun and it's one that if you master will almost certainly enhance your sex life. Did you get that?

Will almost

certainly

enhance

your sex life.

Read it and weep *Hello! Magazine*.

But of course sex as an act is separate from your sexual life force, your creative sexual centre, your own personal sexuality which is your core being, what Gurdjieff described as your essence, your innate self.

And *that*...

Is where we're going next.

* * *

Remember that sexually speaking, there is no normal.

Don't trust what you read about sex in glossy magazines –
talk to people.

Forget what they taught you in religious studies.

Risk being vulnerable.

Ignore your inner critic.

Sex is NOT SHAMEFUL.

Be as sexy as you are.

Master the art of self-pleasuring – it's not dirty.

Observe yourself lovingly.

Chapter 9

This Thing's Bigger Than the Both of Me

By the way if anyone here is in advertising or marketing... kill yourself.

No, no, no it's just a little thought. I'm just trying to plant seeds. Maybe one day, they'll take root – I don't know. You try, you do what you can. Kill yourself. Seriously though, if you are, do. You are Satan's spawn filling the world with bile and garbage. You are fucked and you are fucking us. Kill yourself. It's the only way to save your fucking soul, kill yourself.
Bill Hicks said that...

We are not old men – we are not concerned with your petty morals.
Keith Richards said that...

It's difficult to believe in yourself because the idea of self is an artificial construction. You are, in fact, part of the glorious oneness of the universe. Everything beautiful in the world is within you.
Russell Brand said that...

Marilyn Monroe wasn't even her real name, Charles Manson isn't his real name, and now, I'm taking that to be my real name. But what's real? You can't find the truth, you just pick the lie you like the best.
Marilyn Manson said that...

All I can do is be me, whoever that is.
Bob Dylan said that...

You must understand that every man has two completely separate parts, as it were two different men, in him. These are his essence and his personality.

Essence is I – it is our heredity, type, character, nature.

Personality is an accidental thing – upbringing, education, points of view – everything external. It is like the clothes you wear, your artificial mask, the result of your upbringing, of the influence of your surroundings, opinions consisting of information and knowledge, which change daily, one annulling the other.

Essence does not change.

Here, when we speak of development and change, we speak of essence.

The point is to re-establish what has been lost, not to acquire anything new. This is the purpose of development. For this, one must learn to discriminate between essence and personality.

From *Views from the Real World: Early Talks of Gurdjieff in Moscow.*

I'm wearing Levis Vintage Clothing 1947 Big E 501 jeans, constructed in Turkey, hand distressed in Italy and made from red selvage, 12oz. Cone Mills denim from North Carolina. Underneath I sport a pair of simple white Calvin Klein cotton boxers. Up top it's a Levi's Vintage Clothing 1960s Striped Tee Yellow Stripe beneath a Levi's Vintage Clothing 1950s Crew Sweatshirt in Medieval Blue.

My analyst once told me I have a jeans fetish – what the fuck does he know? He couldn't tell a Flat Head 3001 from a Studio D'Artisan SD-103. I, however, wouldn't be seen dead in anything but Levis Vintage.

Apart from all the ink that progressively adorns my body I also have a silver Berber ring from Essaouira on my left hand, a Calavera Mexican skull ring on my right, accompanied by a genuine eleventh-century Crusader's ring on my little finger.

On my right-hand wrist I have sandalwood mala beads and a multicoloured Tibetan skull bracelet; on my left a Suunto Core All Black Watch, which – as you'll no doubt be aware – is a tried and tested favourite among premium outdoor activity watches.

With the combination of powerful environmental sensors and advanced computer wrist-top technology, it boasts high-performance functionality. I love the technical data such as altitude, air pressure and air temperature, which are available at the press of a button and an in-built compass which ensures the Suunto Core *truly* is an all-round and practical outdoors activity watch. And apart from the fact it's a piece of shit and none of the functions really work, that is if you can actually fathom exactly *how* to work the fucking thing in the first place, I really like it because a) it suggests I'm a rugged outdoorsy type and b) it makes me look cool.

Around my neck I'm wearing a simple string of love beads bought from a stall in the central bazaar in Pondicherry, or 'Pondi' if you're a white hippy middle-class Condé Nast traveller.

Right now I'm barefoot but if I go out I'll slip into a pair of camouflage pattern Reef flip flops which have a really comfortable, water-friendly synthetic nubuck upper, contoured compression moulded EVA foot-bed with anatomical arch support, Full 360^0 heel airbag enclosed in soft polyurethane and – dig this – hidden beneath the foot arch a bottle opener so that you can casually pop the top from a Corona and look incredibly cool and amuse your mates and impress chicks and coat the mouth of your beer bottle in dog shit.

And so, if you buy all of these products, you can be just like me.

Which begs a really difficult question.

Who the fuck am I?

And just before you go, *'ah ha! I knew the silly bastard didn't have a clue what he was talking about – he doesn't even know who he is,'* ask yourself the same question?

Can you answer it? *Really?*

Yeah…

Not so easy is it fancy-pants?

And sure, you'd be forgiven for saying, *'well… it's* me *isn't it,*

I'm _____, I'm a forty-seven-year-old pipe fitter from Bounds Green, that's who I am.'

Really? Is your *name* who you are? Your age? Your job?

My job, not that I consider what I do to be a job, it's too much fun, is what I *do*, some of the time, which I guess comes from my amassed life experiences, the way my brain functions, my level of intuition, my creativity, all aspects of *how* rather than *who* I am, and only *aspects*.

My age you could say is a biological situation based on an intellectual concept called time, a linear measuring system that leaves me somehow unconvinced, for as Janis Joplin said, *"as a matter of fact, as we discovered in the train, tomorrow never happens, man. It's all the same fucking day, maaaan..."* At least Bob had a clue when he observed that, *"he not busy bein' born is busy dyin'"*. My age may be how long I've been here, but it's not *who* I am.

And my name is a sound attached to me by someone else, attached to me before they even knew me. And it never helped me have a sense of self, too many people had too many ideas as to what I should be called – to my father I was Jeremy, and, therefore, usually only used when I was in the shit. To my mother, when I wasn't in the shit, I was Jem. To my Grandparents I was James or Jim, the name I actually have most resonance with, because of the quality of the relationship. To my friends, enemies and teachers at my first school I was called Hyde. At senior school I was Jerry for the first time. To my band mates I was Deke Tremelo.

There's a lot attached to a name – think about it: what's yours? Who gave it to you? What was their agenda? What energy does it have for you, do you like it, and does it fit?

But it's not *who* you are.

Sri Nisargadatta Maharaj nailed it, in *I AM That*:

Give up all questions except one: Who am I? After all, the only fact that you are sure of is that you are. The 'I am' is certain. The 'I am this' is not. Struggle to find out what you are in reality.

Then there are those fun games like, who would play you in a movie of your life? Someone suggested Alan Alda for me, but he simply doesn't have the skill, depth or gravitas to play the role. No, I'd require the presence, commitment and *dignity* of Daniel Day Lewis, or perhaps if he was resting, Christian Bale.

And I want Cimino to direct.

Who would play you? And what would they be trying to capture, to portray?

And portray here is the operative word 'cos we're all playing a character.

All the world's a stage, and all the men and women merely players: they have their exits and their entrances; and one man in his time plays many parts.

Shakespeare was a clever bastard...

In *'In Search of the Miraculous'*, the definitive book on Gurdjieff, P.D. Ouspensky said more about essence and personality:

a very important moment in the work on oneself is when a man begins to distinguish his personality and his essence.

A man's real I, his individuality, can grow only from his essence. It can be said that a man's individuality is his essence, grown up, mature.

But in order to enable essence to grow up, it is first of all necessary to weaken the constant pressure of personality upon it, because the obstacles to the growth of essence are contained in personality.

Osho made more or less the same point when he said,

you ask me: what happened when you became enlightened?

I laughed, a real uproarious laugh, seeing the whole absurdity of trying to be enlightened. The whole thing is ridiculous because we are born enlightened, and to try for something that is already the case is the most absurd thing. If you already have it, you cannot achieve it; only those things can be achieved which you don't have, which are not intrinsic parts of your being. But enlightenment is your very nature.

Gurdjieff in turn went on to say,

a man must die, that is, he must free himself from a thousand petty attachments and identifications which hold him in the position in which he is. He is attached to everything in his life, attached to his imagination, attached to his stupidity, attached even to his suffering, possibly to his sufferings more than to anything else. He must free himself from this attachment. Attachment to things, identification with things, keep alive a thousand useless I's in a man. These I's must die in order that the big I may be born.

And so we are back yet again to enlightenment, self-realisation.

Remember?

And there is a real dilemma here; because we've created a society in which to be enlightened creates certain problems. Indeed, to the Western perception there is often a fine line between enlightenment and insanity.

Sadhu Amar Bharati is an Indian holy man who has kept his right hand raised in the air since 1973. David Deida, author of *Finding God Through Sex* (never read it, couldn't tell you what it's about) made the point that in India, Amar Bharati has become a symbol for Shiva worshipers all around the nation but try a stunt like that in downtown LA and fairly soon you'd find yourself in a 'secure' unit.

But we mustn't forget that there is a positive function of the personality, which takes us back to the fear of exile, in that our persona is our ticket to belonging. I remember as far back as 1969 when in order to be in with the 'in' crowd in the playground the price of admission was a pair of Clark's Commandos which were actually just plain bog standard black lace-up school shoes but... and this was the brilliant part... they had a C on the side of the heel.

Which meant you fucking ROCKED.

And not much else.

But this was a small building brick in what was to become the fortress that I understood to be me. The clothes I wore; the music I listened to; the way I cut my hair (*"Daddy – why did you have hair like a pink chicken when you were at art school?"* Just one of those unanswerable questions that I have to live with); the cars I drive; the way I furnish my home; my website... It goes on and on, and all gives me a sense of place, of belonging. Of safety.

It feels like a big risk, a lot to let go of in order to find your essence. And if I threw away all of these things, how would my friends know me, how would I relate to them (especially if they threw away their packaging). It would be like going to a super-market where none of the cans had labels – how would I know which was beans and which was dog food?

To be who you really are takes big balls, fearlessness, and a strong sense of self. Ironically, it's been by looking, creatively, at my projections onto others that I have deepened my connection to who *seems* to be me; and I use the word seems there deliber-ately. It's by recognising the common denominators that unite my heroes, Keith Richards, Hunter S. Thompson and Bill Hicks that I have come closer to my own essence.

And the key ingredient? The unifying factor?

They don't give a *fuck* what anyone thinks of them. They're outspoken, opinionated and fearless in their delivery, which feels very true to who I am at my core, and very different to the fragile and terrified youth who emerged from art school wearing the leather uniform of a rock and roller to disguise the complete absence of any kind of self-confidence.

Ironically, I was pretending to the world that I didn't give a *fuck* what anyone thought of me and that if I opened my mouth I'd probably be outspoken, opinionated and fearless in my delivery.

And it kind of worked.

Letting go of all my packaging, my labels, my armour is still clearly too much for me, otherwise I wouldn't be so hung up on Cone Mills Denim. Getting divorced shed a big layer, being publically outed as an adulterer dulled a lot of that hard-earned respectable coating but to give it all up – no, I'm still a way off that, but with every part of my true essence that I wake up to, another piece of the personality crumbles.

And for most of us that's probably the way to do it.

Nature is a wonderful teacher if you take the time to notice. Sadly for most of us it's become an enemy, something to hide from behind double-glazed windows in centrally heated air-conditioned artificially illuminated boxes called homes.

But if you do ever venture out of your box there are a million miracles available to those who pause long enough.

I learned a great lesson on an Enlightenment Intensive run by Shivam O'Brien in Wales recently.

(An Enlightenment Intensive is a beautiful process using the self-enquiry meditation method popularised by Ramana Maharshi of paying constant attention, over a period of days, to the inner awareness of 'I'. It's designed to enable a spiritual enlightenment experience within a relatively short time and it can, and often does, give a glimpse of Nirvana, or as a friend of mine put it, *"it's like coming up on a pill."*

Bless...

From the sacred to the profane – but then how can there be one without the other?)

Anyway, I was sitting by a river trying and failing to stop my

FUCKING MIND from running riot through my entire *being* and I looked down and there was the most beautiful slate stone at my feet. Now I should point out that I was in a remote Welsh valley where slate stones are not exactly rare but there was something magical about this one that called to me, something about its shape, its colour, its presence...

And so, forgetting all notions of paying constant attention to the inner awareness of 'I', I reached down and picked up the precious prize from where it protruded from the mud.

And it crumbled into a dozen pieces in my hand.

I was mortified.

I felt like a thief, a clumsy burglar, a vandal in the British Museum running amuck with a sledgehammer, like I'd destroyed an ancient and priceless artefact... (I *was* three days into the Intensive at this point remember...)

As if it were a small bird whose skeleton I'd unwittingly crushed, I looked down at the broken pieces in dismay. Fuck – this rock had been intact for millions of years until this moment, until I happened upon it wreaking destruction and, er... destruction.

And it was I, yes *I* that had broken this precious... this precious, er... *thing* into pieces, never again would it be intact, never again would it be whole, its fragments separated for all time, never again to be united – and all because...

Of *me*.

Then a little voice in my head – let's call this voice *sanity* shall we? A little voice said, *"bullshit."*

"Huh?"

"Bullshit."

"What do you mean bullshit? I'm a... I'm a rock killer."

"You're talking arrogant, self-important, melodramatic bullshit."

"Shut up, I'm not..."

"How the fuck do you imagine that rock got to be that shape, genius? Huh? Didn't actually make it to geography O-Level didja?"

"So what?"

"So go figure. That rock is a smaller part of a much bigger rock that

was a smaller part of a much bigger rock. In fact that rock wasn't even that shape yesterday. That rock has been changing shape for millions of years."

"Oh... I hadn't thought of that."

"If anything, you just assisted that rock to achieve its purpose."

"Really?"

"Yeah, that rock's sole purpose, that rock's soul purpose, is to become smaller and smaller and smaller until it's returned to the subatomic particles of which it was originally formed. That rock's mission... Is to not exist."

"To not..."

"That's right Einstein. To not exist. Just... Like... Everything... Else."

BOOOM!

Okay, mebbe you had to be there, but it woke me *right* up. Shit – it's true, this is where we're all heading, this is the mission, we're all in a process of disintegration, this is what Gurdjieff is talking about when he says *'a man must die, that is, he must free himself from a thousand petty attachments and identifications which hold him in the position in which he is.'*

George – I'm ready man, I'm ready to let go, I'm ready to transcend these petty desires, these shallow attachments, these masks, these pretences, I'm ready to be real, to live from my heart, to speak from my soul, to flow from the one true source.

I'M READY GEORGE, I'M READY...

Can I just keep the car?

* * *

Give up all questions except, "who am I?"

Who would play you in the biopic of your life?

Distinguish between your personality and your essence.

Remember – enlightenment is your very nature, let go of as much of your packaging as you can.

Observe yourself lovingly.

Chapter 10

The Brown Acid Isn't Specifically
Too Good...

I wouldn't recommend sex, drugs or insanity for everyone, but they've always worked for me.
Hunter S. Thompson said that...

If you want to fight a war on drugs, sit down at your own kitchen table and talk to your own children.
Barry McCaffrey said that...

I don't do drugs. I am drugs.
Salvador Dali said that...

They lie about marijuana. Tell you pot-smoking makes you unmotivated. Lie! When you're high, you can do everything you normally do just as well — you just realize that it's not worth the fucking effort. There is a difference.
Bill Hicks said that...

Let me be clear about this. I've never had a problem with drugs. I've had a problem with policemen.
Keith Richards said that...

The Dalai Lama said something very interesting about drugs. He was asked, *"So – what's the deal with psychedelics? Do they offer instant enlightenment?"* And he replied, *"fuck yeah!"* (I'm paraphrasing), *"but unless you've done fifteen to twenty years of meditative practice and spiritual work it won't do shit man, you just won't be able to process what you get – there are no short cuts dawg – you feelin' me?"*

And he's right of course. In my time, apart from LSD 25, I've conducted extensive and *exhaustive* research, with little or no concern for my own safety, into opium, methadone, Moroccan double zero hashish, Lebanese pollen, Himalayan Charas, Kerala grass, opiated Nepalese Temple Balls, Filipino hash oil, Dutch Skunk, Thai weed, Mexican weed, African bush, Jamaican ganja, Pro Plus, blue speed, pink speed, green speed, yellow speed, nitrous oxide, GHB, amyl nitrate, MDMA, ecstasy, cocaine, crack cocaine, Valium, Librium, Codeine, Phenodihydrochloride Benzelex, Dexedrine, Ritalin, Benylin with Jack Daniels on the side, psilocybin mushrooms, psychedelic truffles, nutmeg, and various other unnamed and unidentifiable uppers, downers, screamers, laughers and sidewinders.

I never took heroin 'cos I didn't want to develop a drug problem (yeah) but I had a pretty good time on the rest of them.

But I never got enlightened.

I had an interesting 'ethical' dilemma recently when a client of mine asked if I'd recommend that he drop acid.

Hmmmmmmmmmmmmmmmmmmmmm...

And what I ended up saying is that I wouldn't recommend that anyone drop acid, I would recommend that everyone *had* dropped acid. Which you could say was a cop out, but what I meant was that whilst I prize my experiences with LSD above almost all others – fuck me it was a close call. I mean, I *saw* the doors of perception and they were hanging on some very rusty looking hinges, the paint was all flaking off and there was a bloody handprint on the dirty window pane and something unspeakable was oozing through the keyhole and I *knew* that what lay behind was far too dark for me to explore.

At that stage...

In his book on masculinity, *He*, the Jungian writer Robert A. Johnson says that Parcifal's failure to find the Grail on his first visit to the Fisher King's castle symbolises the growth opportunities that as teenagers we are unable to embrace. He states that they return to us in midlife when we are more able to understand them. I feel this is a similar thing that the Dalai is saying – you have to be ready, you have to have put in the hours. I remember laying on the floor at about four o'clock in the morning in my flat off the King's Road and I got it, I mean I absolutely *got* the meaning of life, death, the universe and beyond with absolute clarity and totality.

And could I remember it the next morning?

Could I fuck.

And so I had to go out and make the same mistakes over and over and learn the hard way until they gradually worked their way into my consciousness.

And from the tone of this chapter you may have already established that I'm not entirely anti-drugs, and you'd be right, I believe the war of drugs is utterly ludicrous and that all, yes all, narcotics should be decriminalised and the money spent fighting this bullshit war should be redirected into educating people about the very real dangers of drugs, because although I'm not anti-drugs, I'm very anti-drug abuse.

The next section I like to call –

When drugs go bad!

A friend of mine took the powerful plant medicine Dimethyltryptamine (DMT) – which, along with ayahuasca, I'm currently considering adding to my CV – in a squat in Willesden. The experience was rather far from sacred and involved him being ushered from a brightly lit waiting room into an office where all his ancestors and spirit guides were sitting behind a desk. They took one look at him and said, *"how dare you come in here like that?"* and he woke up having shat himself, covered in vomit, and feeling rejected on the most profound spiritual level imaginable. Took him about six months to straighten back out.

Next a less traumatic drug story that's become part of urban myth but that I personally know to be true because it happened to my friend Hugh Mackenzie.

Hugh is a young, delicate, Kenneth Williams lookalike who decided that it would be a really great idea to take acid for the first time while house-sitting for his parents in Cornwall.

Not having a clue what to expect, once the acid kicked in Hugh was taken with an overwhelming *need* to drive, and so it was that he found himself hurtling down the fast lane of the motorway in his father's car at about three o'clock in the morning.

The road was empty and Hugh described the experience as not at all dissimilar to piloting an X-Wing Fighter into the Death Star, his knuckles white against the steering wheel, arms taught, brow furrowed, eyes bulging, *total focus.*

Which is when he saw the blue flashing light in his rear view mirror.

Having taken his details the policeman asked Hugh, *"have you any idea just how fast you were driving sir?"*

"Er... I can't say that I was looking at the speedometer officer but I'm sure I wasn't going much more than seventy-five at a push?"

"No..."

"Eighty?"

"Try again sir..."

"Well there's no way I was driving faster than eighty-five officer, I'm sure of that."

"Mr Mackenzie – you were driving at seventeen miles an hour..."

My own nightmare came unexpectedly one Sunday afternoon. I'd retired, not for the first time, to the Prince Charles Cinema off Leicester Square to quietly munch a blotter of acid and watch *Apocalypse Now*. It's the perfect acid movie – you drop it on the way in, by the time you're coming up you're at the helicopter scene, then you've got all the fireworks and visuals at the Do Lung Bridge and by the time Marlon starts banging on about snails crawling along straight razors you've peaked and it all *makes sense...*

Only thing was, on that particular Sunday when I emerged from the theatre wild eyed and grinding my teeth from too much strychnine in the acid, no one had told me it was Chinese New Year and there were fireworks going off and Oriental people in black pyjamas running around everywhere and suddenly I was back in Saigon...

The point being – have some *respect* people!

And, by the way, my definition of a drug or alcohol problem is pretty hardcore. And I've heard all the excuses too – *'hey man, it's not as if I'm sitting in a pool of my own piss drinking meths out of a brown paper bag round the back of Piccadilly...'*

Sure – there's always someone worse than us who we can compare ourselves to in order to feel better or superior.

But to my mind, if you're *using* it you're *abusing* it.

It's not about quantity, or even regularity, it's about intention.

If I am totally sober for three hundred and sixty-four days of the year but on the anniversary of my grandfather's death I get totally shit faced because I can't handle the grief then I have a problem. And sure – there's a scale, but like everything else, you've got to have a brutally honest relationship with yourself to really be clean and serene, abstinence don't mean shit if you don't know why you were using a substance.

I didn't smoke a cigarette from the age of twenty-three to forty-three. And then I tried one and *boom*, back on thirty a day. Which then took me another six years to kick and made me realise that I hadn't actually kicked it the first time round, I'd just been holding my breath for twenty years. In the end I stopped because I realised how powerful cigarettes were in containing my emotions and I was ready to grow and feel more. Then the tobacco ceased to be an issue.

It wasn't down to patches.

These substances, and I'm including that very sacred herb tobacco, were never intended as party drugs. They were used ceremonially, administered by a medicine man who *knew his shit*.

Siberian shamans used to eat the fly agaric mushroom and the villagers would then drink his piss 'cos the pure mushroom was just too goddamned strong for most people. It's hard to find a dealer like that these days.

I was truly blessed the first time I dropped acid when my man sold it to me on the condition – all included in the one-pound cover charge – that I let him stay with my friends and me all night as a guide. He's a doctor now and I hope he gets an MBE 'cos he did me a huge favour. Doing *any* of these drugs without guidance is akin to 'having a go' at skydiving with a homemade parachute.

I include skunk in this warning by the way. GOD DID NOT PUT SKUNK ON THIS PLANET.

And what's more:

SKUNK IS
SHIT

And to all those contemporaries of mine who say, *'oh lighten up man, it's just a bit of weed – let the kids have some fun, we used to do that back in the day,'* I say a) Don't EVER use the phrase *back in the day* when talking to me, it's stupid and I don't know what it means; and b) the little stalks of Mexican weed or Jamaican sensi we used to get were *not* the same drug as skunk, skunk is a hybrid monster cooked up in the labs by deranged bread head Dutch drug dealers who have ultimately saturated the market – i.e. your children – with a high potency psychoactive drug that's almost as strong as acid.

And sure, you might counter and call me a hypocrite by taking LSD in the past and I'd say to you I KNEW I was taking a risk with acid. I knew the likelihood was that it'd been cooked up in the back of a van on a slip-road off the M25 by a bunch of pikeys who cut it with strychnine, and so I was always on alert for any potential problems. But Skunk is sold as a 'soft' drug – which it isn't – which suggests that it's innocuous and benign. Which it isn't. And all these kids having psychotic reactions? It's because skunk massively inhibits your dream function and if you don't dream you don't process anything and if you don't process anything...

You go mad.

Simple.

I was born at the tail end of the baby boom, into a world that was a very frightened, frightening and conservative place with Kennedy dead and the Cold War raging with a populace desperately trying to smile in the face of nuclear extinction. LSD literally changed the consciousness of the planet, instigated the anti-war and anti-nuclear movements and arguably played a major role in bringing us back from the brink. The dust had long settled and the hippie ideals morphed into proto yuppies by the time I first took acid. But, nevertheless, although I *forgot* the meaning of life, it opened me up to the possibility that there might be something much, much more to life than the way my middle-class upbringing had suggested. It set me on the path; the first step beyond the walls of Camelot and after that there was no going back.

Likewise, MDMA changed the world – look at football hooliganism in the UK before and after that one hit the terraces. As Jarvis sang, *'everybody asks your name, they say we're all the same and it's "nice one, geezer", but that's as far as the conversation went...'*

But no one stabbed anyone on ecstasy.

Just like LSD, MDMA escaped from the labs where it's now once again, in California of course, being used very effectively in the treatment of war veterans suffering from post-traumatic stress disorder. And do I accept that these substances could be used to assist people in their healing?

I believe you know me well enough by now to know the answer to that.

And as a Gonzo therapist, would I *do* it?

Hell yeah, in the right circumstances (which prohibition makes difficult in terms of drug quality and medical safety) and with the right person – but don't tell anyone, I'd hate for it to get out and my reputation is already shot.

Am I worried about my kids growing up and taking drugs? Damned right I am, but not so much the taking of the drugs but more the quality and circumstances. Kids die on drugs like MDMA as a rule because of two things; the environment – a night club might be fun (my idea of hell) but it's not a safe place to mess with your head, and because of what the drugs are cut with. In some clubs in Holland you can go get your pill tested to see just what you're taking, and it's a fact that most heroin addicts who die do so because they suddenly get a really pure batch of uncut smack and overdose because they don't realise just how good the shit is.

However, one of the main reasons I quit drugs was because I started to resent them, I didn't want to be dependent on a substance or chemical to evoke an experience, I wanted to be able to get there myself. And remember. So I went to India, got some therapy – you know the rest of the story...

And now, after all these years, I'm doing all that I can to remember what I forgot, what we all forget, to just be, to observe without judgement. Because of course if you watch a baby for just five minutes, you'll see that's what they do. We are born with the ability to just sit...

And be.

There's a lot of thought out there that suggests what we now call enlightenment, an experience of oneness with all things, used to be our default way of being, but then our population swelled, we moved into being city dwellers and forgot our true nature. Babies haven't had time to forget (what Gurdjieff was really urging us to do with self-remembering was to recall what we once knew – enlightenment may seem far from your grasp but the fact is – *you've already been there*. As Osho said, *"enlight-enment is your very nature…"*) But then someone decides that there are lots of important things for us to do and experience and learn and attempt and conquer and explore and achieve and we forget who we once were and become driven and confused and clever and depressed and end up, if we don't die of some stress related illness, sitting in an old people's home just sitting and being.

Full circle.

You wrote the story, remember?

Bill Hicks said something similar long ago:

It's time for a new philosophy, folks. One based on, yes, the principles of Jesus which were love your brother as yourself because, you know what? He IS yourself. Literally. Ha ha ha ha ha ha ha! We are literally all one. Okay. The body is an illusion, cuz God doesn't create things that can be destroyed cuz he's God! Dig it? We have miscreated this world. It's a dream. What's that old song? Row, row, row your boat, gently down the stream, merrily, merrily, merrily, merrily, life is but a dream. You see, we knew it as children. We forgot it.

Way ahead man, way ahead.

* * *

Remember – there are no shortcuts.

Treat drugs with respect and if you're going to do them preferably do so with a guide.

If you're using it you're abusing it.

Observe yourself lovingly.

Chapter 11

The Secret of Success

Perseverance.

Chapter 12

Eat. Shit. Die.

We shall not cease from exploration, and the end of all our exploring will be to arrive where we started and know the place for the first time.
T. S. Eliot said that...

Now this is not the end. It is not even the beginning of the end. But it is, perhaps, the end of the beginning.
Winston Churchill said that. Presumably... when pissed.

Before enlightenment, chop wood and carry water.
After enlightenment, chop wood and carry water.
Some Zen dude said that...

But better die than live mechanically a life that is a repetition of repetitions.
D. H. Lawrence said that...

Of course, like anybody I repeat myself endlessly, but I don't know that I'm doing it, usually.
Brian Eno said that...

And in the end, the love you take, is equal to the love you make.
The Beatles said that...

Dave! For fuck's sake, stop being so fucking fucked up!
I said that. Apparently...

The world is like a ride at an amusement park, and when you choose to go on it, you think it's real, because that's how powerful our minds are. *And the ride goes up and down and round and round and it has thrills and chills and it's very brightly coloured and it's very loud. And it's fun, for a while.*

Some people have been on the ride for a long time, and they begin to question: 'Is this real? Or is this just a ride?' And other people have remembered, and they come back to us and they say 'Hey! Don't worry, don't be afraid – ever – because... this is just a ride.'

And we kill those people.

William Melvin "Bill" Hicks
December 16, 1961 – February 26, 1994

Or, put it another way:

I know nothing about it all and see not difference between you and me. My life is a succession of events, just like yours. Only I am detached and see the passing show as a passing show, while you stick to things and move along with them.

Sri Nisargadatta Maharaj, *I Am That*.

So – this is the end of this part of the ride, of this part of the show.

But what is the end? That always hurt my brain, trying to imagine the end of the universe, there must be a brick wall there or something and if so what's behind the brick wall and anyway what does it *mean* – infinite? Or do they mean full circle – you go far enough out into space, you end up back where you started. And now I'm starting to sound like Dennis Hopper in Apocalypse, *"you can't travel in space, you can't go out into space, you know, without, like, you know, uh, with fractions – what are you going to land on – one-quarter, three-eighths?"*

But I know what's going through your mind, and you're right, I'm fluffing this (in the literary rather than pornographic sense), I'm just talking shit, stalling for time, I'm avoiding the inevitable...

Ending.

I hate endings.

The late, great family therapist Virginia Satir used to say that every single transition was an ending and required a conscious grieving process, even if it was leaving the house to go to the office in the morning. Which is not to say that you must draw the blinds and wear black but that these moments are worthy of attention, just in the noticing that you are ending something – in this case family time – in order to transition smoothly into a work space.

Few people understand the importance of ending well, and the skill that it requires. I personally consider myself a world expert in ending extremely badly, leaving chaos and disaster in my wake. Good endings generally require consciousness, time – to slow down – and the willingness to feel grief. No wonder then that it doesn't rate highly on people's résumés.

I'd rather run out the door any day. Boarding school required me, in effect, to move house every three months. To and from two cultures, home and school, that absolutely rejected any display of emotion. My mum told me recently that she and my sister would wave, smiling, as my father drove me away, and that when the car had disappeared around the corner they'd both break down in tears. Kind of wished I'd known that at the time, 'cos to me it looked like they were glad to see the back of my sorry ass.

Then, after a two-hour drive in total silence, I'd arrive at school, my dad would shake my hand without looking me in the eye and fuck off as quick as possible and I'd have to go through the pretence of appearing to not give a shit to about five hundred other traumatised kids.

What do you mean traumatised you toffee-nosed public school ponce?

I'll tell you what I mean, although it had to be explained to *me*. I remember talking with enormous guilt to my therapist, Rex Bradley, about the privilege of being public school educated – my grandparents were working-class people who shouted at the TV when the Queen came on and somehow I felt that I'd betrayed them in being sent away to school.

Rex just looked me in the eye and said, *"you know nothing about privilege."*

"I don't?"

"I'll tell you what privilege is. My foster mum raised me in the arse end of Portsmouth in the 1950s. Every day she'd wake me up, make me breakfast and walk me up the end of the road to school. At lunchtime I'd come home and she'd have my favourite home cooked meal on the table and she'd read me stories from my Biggles book. After school I'd go out into the street and play football with my mates until it was time for tea, and after that she'd take me upstairs, bath me and tuck me up in bed and kiss me goodnight. Now that, is privilege..."

I got his point. And sure, I benefitted in a great many ways from my education, but boarding school – although it has evolved over the years – in essence is a colonial throwback, a huge lumbering machine designed to shut young men down emotionally so that they can be sent off to the furthest corners of the Empire to oversee those foreign Johnnies without feeling...

And I'm still untangling that one and that's why good endings are a struggle, and until we WAKE UP to these patterns that were established in our formative years we are cursed to repeat the same mistakes over and over again.

Do you ever get déjà vu? You ever get the feeling... I've been here before? This seems... *familiar*? This ain't cosmic; man – I *rely* on it to make a living, if the people I work with didn't keep doing the same old shit over and over and over again they'd be sorted in about two sessions and I'd be out of a job. And you know what keeps people attached to doing the same old shit? It's the attachment to our persona, that character, that mask that we believed we had to become to be loved and accepted. It's a pair of Levis Vintage Clothing 501s – that is ALL that stands between the divine and me.

And that's not me being cynical, that to me is karma. I didn't really *get* karma before I went to India, but by the time I came back I realised that what they call karma we call SSDD. Same shit different day. And that same shit will keep happening again and again until you learn the lesson that life keeps presenting you with. Eckhart Tolle put it more eloquently in *A New Earth: Awakening to Your Life's Purpose:*

> *Life will give you whatever experience is most helpful for the evolution of your consciousness. How do you know this is the experience you need? Because this is the experience you are having at the moment.*

I love Eckhart, he's 'the bomb' as they'd say in *Breaking Bad*, even if he does look a little bit too much like the really bad Nazi in the first *Raiders of the Lost Ark* film...

You'll have almost certainly recognised from your own life that usually the things that come around again and again and again and again are the *shit* things. How many times have you asked yourself – *why does this keep happening to me?* Which, by the way, it doesn't keep *happening* – you keep *creating* these same patterns.

Same shit different day is a cliché, but I figure anything that's happened enough times to establish itself as a cliché is worth attention. Actually, that's the only real cure – attention. To observe lovingly. I notice that I tend to make a lot of the same mistakes that I made thirty years ago, almost identical sometimes, the difference is that now I get interested, I pay attention to the AFGO, I watch and learn. And things change. Very... very... slowly.

Which, by the fucking *way*, is how we are supposed to operate. RANT ALERT RANT ALERT.

(And also an opportunity for my girlfriend to read this and go, *'hold on – what makes you feel you're qualified to talk about slowing down? Etc. etc....'*)

But it is. Read *The Songlines* by Bruce Chatwin. He makes a very simple point – a baby is crying, what's the best solution? Walk with it. It will soon be calmed.

We are walkers by nature, hunter-gatherers, nomadic wanderers. We've been around in our current form for about two hundred thousand years. We didn't even start using horses until six thousand years ago; that means that for one hundred and ninety-four thousand years – we walked.

THAT'S ONE HUNDRED AND NINETY-FOUR THOUSAND FUCKING YEARS

Wheeled vehicles appeared from the mid 4th millennium BC. The first steam train was built in 1784. We'd been around roughly one hundred and ninety-nine thousand, nine hundred and something years before we first took to the skies.

The point being – we are *supposed* to experience life slowly, but the reality is everything now is about speed and we just can't keep up... with ourselves.

I run courses based on the Native American Vision Quest in which I get people to sit, on their own, in a ten-foot circle without food for four whole days.

Just to give them the experience of *slowing down*.

And personal growth, our own evolution, is a very slow thing requiring a lot of patience, perseverance and the willingness to fail repeatedly.

There's an old saying:

    A work of art isn't finished, it's abandoned

Of course to even quote that, all my creative demons go berserk, *'work of art? You have the gall to even allude to this rambling, incoherent, repetitive, self-indulgent piece of crap as being art? How pretentious can you be?'*

Whatever. I'm gonna use it anyway.

And so – before we abandon ship, *has* there been any new wisdom? For *you*? Maybe. Has there been any *old* wisdom – well I believe there has. My favourite bits have been the quotes. If I had to pick from all the different ones I've used it'd be Cecil Beaton's,

    'be daring, be different, be impractical, be anything that will assert integrity of purpose and imaginative vision against the play-it-safers, the creatures of the commonplace, the slaves of the ordinary.'

That's definitely worth having exhaustive and painful laser surgery to remove all my tats in order to clear enough room to have that one all over my flesh. Or stealing one of those cars that have a huge tannoy on the roof that go round on polling day, and screaming it from the rooftops.

Before we finish, I'd suggest that you have a really good, long, hard look at what you recognise to be the repeated lessons that keep appearing in your life, and maybe... make a list?

Unless suffering is your thing.

You wrote it this way or that way so that your soul could keep experiencing what it needs in order to evolve, but unless you figure out what those chapters are, how are you ever going to work them through with any consciousness?

Shit, you even wrote this book into your life for *some* reason, you wrote that at this point in your development you'd walk into a store or click on a website and buy this book in order to learn whatever it is that you needed to learn. And if you got one tiny scrap of information that helped, then good, if one single line or phrase triggered a new way of looking at things then great, it's been worth it.

Has this book changed you?

The answer to that is yes it has.

Now – that sounds like a very grandiose statement, but the truth is this book has not only changed *you*, it's also changed the course of history.

I knew it, I knew it all along – he is a dangerous wannabe cult leader and despot in the making...

Well maybe I am, but this book...

Has changed the course of the world.

In its own minute and unfathomable way.

But then so does going up to the shops to buy a pint of milk if you get hit by a truck – or if you don't get hit by a truck – because every single decision you make changes the world, and the course of history for all time.

No pressure.

I saw a photo in the papers a few years ago of one of the last

Great War veterans, Albert 'Smiler' Marshall, with his family. And when I say family I mean children, grandchildren, great grandchildren, there must have been over a hundred people gathered around him. It had an impact on me – to see the fruits of one man's union with one woman, in less than a hundred years, all gathered together, it made me realise – if *I* can effect just one person positively in my entire career, the ripples of that inter-action are vast. Like Sean Rowley's uncle's one liner – *"remember Sean, you can do anything you set your mind to"* – it changed the course of history.

I remember a guy coming in one week and saying, *"Jerry – that thing you said last week man, it was amazing, it was just so perceptive, so spot on – it just changed everything."*

And my ego just swelled up like a balloon.

"What was it that I said?"

And when he told me I realised that he'd *totally* misheard me, and for a moment it crossed my mind to correct him but then I thought, *'fuck it – he heard what he needed, it just shows how unimportant I really am.'* And it changed the world.

Now where did we begin? Oh yeah, with John Williams' exercise about meeting yourself as a child. So having read this far, if you could meet mini you, what would you say to him or her?

Mine's resolutely the same: don't trust *anyone* who tells you that they know what's right for you. Trust *yourself* – YOU are the expert.

And I'll always be grateful to Pete and Alice for that one.

But if nothing else, before you put this book down I'd suggest you work your one out – and live it. That's the best recipe for authenticity I know, and a good vaccination against repeating the same mistakes and ending up back where you started.

If you don't want to go round and round in circles you need to make some changes.

And so once you've left Camelot, or can sense that departure is imminent, the best first step on the path to my mind is ask around. And as you approach the exit you'll almost certainly begin to notice people who were previously invisible to you, people who are already beyond the castle walls. Your radar will be attuned – you'll suddenly notice, *'that guy who was always at the pub at lunchtime – he now leaves the office with a yoga mat and he's started to say hello to me in the morning – I might go have a chat...'*

Talk to people – sometimes it will be your closest confidants, but not always – friends and family can feel threatened by the idea of you changing. A guy in one of my men's groups told me why he's been coming for the last thirteen years:

"If I go down the pub, and one of my mates asks me how I'm doing and I go, 'not too good actually, things at home aren't great and I'm feeling really depressed about it,' he's gonna go, 'here you are mate, have a pint.' When I come to the group – even though they're not necessarily people I would have chosen as mates – they understand. The rules are different."

There's this idea that to ask for help is to show weakness – traditionally it was mostly men who thought like that but more and more women are being affected by this cultural isolation. But look around – does anyone who you'd really consider successful do it on their own? (Whether you like or respect them or not isn't the point here). Richard Branson, Steve Jobs, Hilary Clinton, Mick Jagger – do they do it without assistance? Without an army of supporters?

No.

Noel Langley (you won't have heard of him but you'll have *heard* him) is a mate of mine, and one of the greatest trumpet players in the world.

He's a player of trumpets.

That's what he does – better than almost anyone else.

He's really, *really* good at playing – the trumpet.

But he's a really shit plumber. And an even worse accountant. And I wouldn't trust him to service my car.

Amazing at trumpet – shit at many other things.

And I'm not sure how good a trumpet player my accountant is… but, the point being – do what you're good at and get other people to deal with the things you can't – create jobs and become more time-efficient in one swoop.

And most of us aren't that great at sorting out our own heads when we're feeling messed up.

So ask around, find out what the word on the street is as to what people found helpful and supportive. Now I can't get too prescriptive here, it depends on the situation.

You might be really depressed – okay, there's a lot of options with that one. It doesn't necessarily mean you need psychotherapy (or pills for that matter – I'm not saying they don't *ever* help but they're not *Smarties* either and the shareholders at Eli Lilly make a shit load more money every time your GP writes that script – it's business, not care).

If your depression has been going on for years then you might well need to go down the therapy route, but you tell me that your finances are in a mess and you don't know how to do your tax return, I'm gonna tell you to go get an accountant – boom, you're on the road to recovery.

You tell me you're sick, your energy is low and you keep getting colds that you can't shift, probably the first visit should be to your GP. But once all the tests come back blank that's when you start asking around for a good therapist or counsellor.

Point is we all need a good support system, a team, a bunch of people who have got our backs. My accountant is easily as important to me as any therapist I've ever seen, and she's done a lot more for my mental health than many others.

Get the right person for the job.

And you know what – it shocks me how few questions people ever ask when they come in my room for the first time. And okay, they usually come via a recommendation, but do your research and don't be afraid to shop around. At a first meeting with any kind of health practitioner, ask them questions, where did they train, how long have they been practicing, are they in super-vision, are they registered with any kind of governing body?

Ultimately the answers to these questions mean fuck all, they're just pointers. Your instinct, your gut, your intuition is probably the best guide in the situation; I always tell potential clients that at the first consultation, *"go away, digest this meeting, see what your gut tells you – eighty per cent of a good therapeutic relationship is based on chemistry, the remaining twenty per cent is experience, training, expertise etc."*

You won't find me on any psychotherapy register, partly because I don't want to be and partly because they wouldn't have me. Having read this book and picked up on my attitudes you'll probably understand why. Does that mean I'm not right for you? Maybe – but that's for you to decide. Does it mean that someone who is registered is a better therapist than me? Possibly, but that's for you to decide.

It all comes back to YOU.

Psychotherapy is a good starting point, a place to explore and heal some old wounds. Will it be enough? Perhaps, although I'm always a bit disappointed when someone comes to me in crisis and once it's passed they leave. 'Cos I believe that's when things start to get really interesting – that's when you can go deeper than your trauma, that's when spirituality comes into the picture.

But it's your choice – there aren't any rules. Just remember Osho's warning about the three stages of consciousness – ignorant, enlightened and in between. If you do leave Camelot, there's no going back, you can't go part way into the forest and decide you don't really like it and go home...

Most gurus, unsurprisingly, will tell you to find your guru. I don't believe that's such a bad idea, as long as you follow Osho's first commandment. What you define as guru is really down to you – if you get great healing and wisdom from your mechanic every time you're hanging around waiting for an oil change – he's the man for you.

Ask around. Explore. Enquire.

And just because your mate had the most amazing, life-changing, enlightening time with this therapist or that healer or that workshop or on that retreat doesn't mean it's the right one for you.

Ask around. Explore. Enquire.

There are good people out there.

As for me, based on my own experiences, I'd recommend... very little. But then I'm picky. When I first met Shivam O'Brien I remember being quite intimidated by his presence and so when I introduced myself I tried to impress him.

"Yeah, I do some quite out there stuff y'know? Like vision quests 'n stuff – I get people to starve for four days on their own in the woods."

He narrowed his eyes and said:

"Yeah I used to do vision quests – but nowadays I like to do things where there's a real chance that people won't come back..."

And I thought, *'I've found my man...'*

It's whatever speaks to you.

Workshops are good for more intense doses and deeper exploration of specific issues, but be wary of those that promise life-changing results in a weekend. I'm not saying that it's not possible, or that they don't exist, just remember that it's YOU that does the work, it's not like going in for an operation. And the work usually starts when you go home and you have to integrate the learning into your life. I always say that about any of my workshops – they begin when you walk through the door afterwards.

If you can find a good tantra teacher that's a great step out of the comfort zone for most of us. Again ask around, there are some good people out there.

Vision Quests are pretty good, I don't know why, and that's what I love about them – it's not a head-trip, there's still a bit of mystery about them and they're extremely transformative and powerful. But only if the time is right for you. Chances are, if you're interested in something as *out there* as a Vision Quest then the time is right, but take a moment to talk it through with the leader before sending your cheque.

At this stage Enlightenment Intensives are my thing, the deepest, most powerful process I've ever encountered – in ways I struggle to describe – like looking in a mirror and peeling off the layers of who you thought you were as you go deeper and deeper into the truth and beyond.

There was a book that came out a few years ago called *The Okinawa Way* about the Japanese island which has the longest-lived population in the world with very low instances of heart disease, breast cancer, prostate cancer and Alzheimer's. They did a twenty-five-year study to see how come these people were still cycling to work aged one hundred and fifteen.

I guess those of us who read it hoped that it was all going to be down to some magic bean. But it wasn't.

It was down to their entire way of being – the fact they ate a low-fat, low-calorie, high fibre diet was a factor, but so was their exercise regime, their spiritual practice and beliefs, and perhaps most of all their sense of community, of belonging to a tribe.

I've finally, after all these years of searching, found my spiritual home – and even happiness – at the Spirit Horse Community in Mid Wales. They *really* are the tribe from the ledge beyond the edge, and it's not for everyone or the faint-hearted, but their attempts to rebuild culture and provide community in the old sense of the world has filled a gap for me that I became aware of when I first realised I was in exile.

As Shivam wrote to me when I first contacted him about Spirit Horse, *"come sit by our fire – there's a place for you, it's been there a long time"*.

There's a place for you too, somewhere, perhaps where you least expect to find it – do *not* cease searching, night and day, your tribe's out there, somewhere – and they've been waiting a long time. As we explored in the last chapter – it all comes down to perseverance, you keep going long enough and you'll find the Grail, or enlightenment or whatever it is you're seeking.

It's a simple formula – just remember:

"If you're going to try, go all the way. There is no other feeling like that. You will be alone with the gods, and the nights will flame with fire. You will ride life straight to perfect laughter. It's the only good fight there is."

Okay, I know, I know, this chapter's already about eight times longer than the others – I have to end this, I have to let you go – it's me, it's not you, you're a good person, but I told you at the start there were no promises. And yeah I *know* you began this book with good intentions, we both did, with all the hopes and dreams of what it might bring – and a book is like a relationship – you start out full of hope, excitement and expectation, checking out the exterior, the cover, then maybe spending a bit of time flicking through a few pages, testing the water, looking for signs that it has substance and intrigue until slowly you get drawn in and…

* * *

Remember what Bill said; it's just a ride – slow down and enjoy it.

All transitions are endings and require a period of conscious grieving.

Life will give you whatever experience you most need.

You will keep creating the same events in your story until you no longer need them – notice the repeating plot points.

Discover your life's purpose and change the world in your own small way.

Ask for help and get your team together.

Find your tribe.

And always –
Observe…
Yourself…
Lovingly.

Suggested Further Reading and Other Great Shit

Books

Meetings with Remarkable Men by George Gurdjieff

In Search of the Miraculous: The Definitive Exploration of G. I. Gurdjieff's Mystical Thought and Universal View... by P. D. Ouspensky

Intimacy by Osho

Tantra by Osho

Anything at all by Osho

Love All the People by Bill Hicks

I Am That: Talks with Sri Nisargadatta Maharaj by Sri Nisargadatta Maharaj, Sudhakar S. Dikshit and Maurice Frydman

Fear and Loathing in Las Vegas by Hunter S. Thompson

The Three Dangerous Magi: Osho, Gurdjieff, Crowley by P. T. Mistlberger

The Power of Now: A Guide to Spiritual Enlightenment by Eckhart Tolle

She: Understanding Feminine Psychology by Robert A Johnson

He: Understanding Masculine Psychology by Robert A. Johnson

Owning Your Own Shadow: Understanding the Dark Side of the Psyche by Robert A. Johnson

Ecstasy: Understanding the Psychology of Joy by Robert A. Johnson

The Fisher King and the Handless Maiden: Understanding The Wounded Feeling Function In Masculine And Feminine... by Robert A. Johnson

Screw Work, Let's Play: How to Do What You Love and Get Paid for it by John Williams

Storming Heaven: LSD and the American Dream by Jay Stevens

Daring Greatly: How the Courage to Be Vulnerable Transforms

the Way We Live, Love, Parent, and Lead by Brené Brown

Path To Love: Spiritual Lessons for Creating the Love You Need by Dr Deepak Chopra

The Shadow Effect: Illuminating the Hidden Power of Your True Self by Deepak Chopra

Way of the Superior Man by David Deida

It's a Guy Thing: An Owner's Manual for Women by David Deida

Wild Nights: Conversations with Mykonos about Passionate Love, Extraordinary Sex, and How to Open to God by David Deida

Mating in Captivity by Esther Perel

The Heart of Tantric Sex by Diana Richardson

Tantric Lovers: The Ultimate Guide: Making Your Relationship Last by Hanna Katz-Jelfs. I've not read this but I've done some good weekend workshops with Hanna and her husband Martin so I'd expect it's worth a look.

The Okinawa Way: How to Improve Your Health and Longevity Dramatically by Andrew Weil, Bradley J. Willcox, Makoto Suzuki and Craig D. Willcox

The Top Five Regrets of the Dying: A Life Transformed by the Dearly Departing by Bronnie Ware

Film, TV & Music

Performance (1970) directed by Donald Cammell, Nicolas Roeg, starring James Fox, Mick Jagger, Anita Pallenberg

Apocalypse Now (1979) directed by Francis Ford Coppola, starring Martin Sheen, Marlon Brando, Robert Duvall, Dennis Hopper

Bill Hicks: Totally Bill Hicks – It's Just A Ride/Revelations [DVD]

Spice World (1997) directed by Bob Spiers, starring Melanie Brown, Emma Bunton, Melanie Chisholm, Geri Halliwell, Victoria Beckham

Woodwoo (2013) written, directed and starring Jonny Phillips
Breaking Bad. Created by Vince Gilligan, starring Bryan
 Cranston, Anna Gunn, Aaron Paul
Rant In E-Minor by Bill Hicks
Exile On Main Street by The Rolling Stones
Abbey Road by The Beatles
Edentide by Noel Langley
Beyond The Ragasphere by Debashish Bhattacharya and friends

Links

www.spirithorse.co.uk – gatherings, courses, intensives and
 adventures in Wales and Ireland

www.authenticself.co.uk – enlightenment intensives in Wales
 and Ireland with Shivam O'Brien

www.parvanihall.ie – retreats and events in Galway, Ireland

www.screwworkletsplay.com – If you want to quit your job and
 make a living from doing what you love, John Williams is
 your man

www.diamondjacks.co.uk – go see Darryl Gates if you're serious
 about spiritual growth and want an old school tattoo

www.opencentre.com – one of the longest established centres for
 self-development in the UK

www.nityama.com – Shantam Nityama is the tantra man if you
 can track him down

www.awakeningwithin.org.au – Andrew Barnes trained with
 Nityama, is very good and is more available

www.northerndrum.com – renewed perspective on traditional
 shamanic teachings

www.jerryhyde.co.uk – that's me

Big Ups

Now forgive me, this is erm... Gather. Is this really happening?
Okay, erm... Please wrap up? You have no idea how much I'm not
wrapping up. Okay. Gather. Thank you.
Kate Winslet's Golden Globe acceptance speech...

The acknowledgements section is the really *boring* bit isn't it?

Unless you're in it. It's also kind of the most difficult

to write 'cos there's that constant fear – shit, have I forgotten
anyone? And what about that person who did fuck all but will be
pissed off if I don't include them?

Fuck.

It's a nightmare – maybe I should just *swerve* the whole
acknowledgement section, blame it on the publisher... yeah, I
don't know what happened man, yeah – I put you in there but

they just kind of deleted the whole section, yeah, really *pissed*

me off too y'know, I put a lot of effort into that bit, especially

the bit about *you*...

That might work...
Then again I could just include everyone. Cover all the

bases – cut and paste my Facebook friend list for starters, even
though I've never met half of them and the other half I haven't

seen for thirty years. Jesus... this could be *bad* – just when I
thought I was done, that I'd got away with it, this could turn into

a nightmare of out of control Oscar acceptance speech proportions...

Deep breath.

Okay.

So I guess first off it's a big **thank you** to **Sam**

Mendes and everyone at Universal for giving me this opportunity...

Sorry, wrong speech.

First of all, thank you **John Hunt Publishing** and in particular

Alice Grist at **Soul Rocks** for taking me on, being so positive and encouraging, and allowing me so much creative freedom. Everything I went to Alice with and said, *"er... how would it be if I..."* she just went, "yeah, okay..."

That's *unusual*.

Next I'd like to say thank you to my family who gave me all that I am and all that I value – and by family I mean not just those I know and have known,

Pete and **Alice Muckley**,

my parents **Pat** and **Murray** (who didn't always appreciate my 'creative freedom', sorry...) my sister **Gerry** (yes, my parents called us both J/Gerry – don't even **go** there), but also those who came before, the gamekeepers, the farmers, the coal merchants, the furniture makers, the adventurers and the soldiers who lived and loved and laughed and died and whose genes I carry and whose spirits guide and speak through me.

To my daughters, **Noor** and **Tara**, to whom this book

is dedicated and whose births remain the single greatest events of

my life EVER, I say thank you for your beauty and love and light and joyfulness and spirit and creativity and innocence and wonder. *However* that happened, whatever system meant that *you* were born to *me*... I am overwhelmed with gratitude at the honour that it is to know you.

To their mother **Janan Kubba**... only you know what you mean to me.

To **Shivam O'Brien** I say thank you for your brotherhood and friendship and love and furious passion and poetry and grace

and wild soul and beautiful speech, you're one of a kind and it was well worth waiting almost half a century to meet you.

Nadia Hosein – in some ways you deserve co-author status 'cos without the things you brought into my life this book would never have been written. Thank you for your fiery Kali spirit and furious uncompromising lust for life.

Joanne Bernstein and Robert McNab thank you SO much for your generosity, support and love and for hooking me up with **Mr Crumb**, which is like the best icing on any cake. Ever.

Robert Crumb – not only for being so generous as to do the cover but for a lifetime of playing from your fucking heart, for *never* compromising, and for being one of the Gonzo crusaders who showed me *the way*.

Steve Annet, my very own Walter White and the first person to read this book and give me *fantastic* notes, thank you for your love and support and clarity and wisdom and courage always.

Melissa Unger you absolute *powerhouse* of creativity –

Melissa Unger named this book, okay? She gets full credit for that even though she'll never

admit it – sometimes you need people like Melissa when you're lost in the dark and chucking ideas around to go, *"stop – that's the one!"* Play from your fucking heart, darling!

My beautiful friend, the mystical girl with the faraway eyes and the only person apart from **Allah** who's perfect, **Claire Heron**, what a treat to have your words in this book...

Jonny Phillips, one of this country's finest actors, you defined my career, without you I'd probably have given it up. Seriously.

Dominic Murcott, the original remarkable, who showed me this shit actually *works*. If only I was a sorted as you, thank you for your unshaking integrity.

John Williams – it's been a helluva ride man, hats off to you for all that you've achieved, thank you for all your encouragement and **inspiration**. (There's a bit near the beginning of this book where I say the reason I wrote it was 'cos 'people' kept asking when I was going to write a book – that was actually *you*. And you probably said it maybe... *twice* over ten years or so? Don't tell anyone.)

Darryl Gates thanks for the ink, the laughs and your absolute commitment to rock and roll, I wear your work with pride.

Sam Roddick. Warrior Princess, Shakti, heyókȟa fellow traveller – I salute you.

Rex Bradley – rest in peace my friend, there is so much of you in this book, thank you for your love and guidance and your giant yet ultimately fragile **heart** – you have a special place alongside my ancestors.

Paul Gates, John Graham, Dave Crane, Noel Langley (Noel's catchphrase is *"you won't have heard of me, but you will have heard me"* because

he's played trumpet with... everyone, and anyway all

that's gonna change pretty soon with the release of his debut album *Edentide* but the fact that you probably haven't heard of him is just another illustration of the *travesty* that is this nation's ATTITUDE towards creativity and the arts and I truly believe this

country should hang its head in SHAME because we

go on and on and *on* about how FUCKING cultured

we are but some of the world's most gifted artistic talents are forced into getting

'REAL JOBS' driving buses and

plastering ceilings and digging ditches and felling TREES just to feed their children because we simply DO NOT SUPPORT

OR EVEN REALLY VALUE THE ARTS IN BRITAIN.)
Where was I?

Oh yeah, Noel Langley, Steve Howse,

Sean Rowley, Kenny Dickinson,

Justin Gibbons – you are truly *remarkable*

men, it's an honour to know you. 'Nuff said.

To my clients, all of whom I'd love to name but in a

rare and uncharacteristic display of appropriate ethical behaviour... I *won't*, THANK YOU THANK YOU THANK YOU a million times for your loyalty and love and dedication and *belief*, for enriching my life and ensuring that I never ever feel like I go to work.

And to the memory of my dear friends **Julian Bolt** and **Carl Poll** – you are part of this book, I know you'd have enjoyed it.

To my tribe, to **Sue Angel**, **Emily Belfrage** and everyone at Spirit Horse in Wales and beyond, magical, wild people, honest people, people from the earth who I've known for such a relatively short time and yet who I've known always, I've learned so much – thank you for my place by your fire.

Thank you **Ian Mackenzie** for a lifetime's friendship and laughter and loyalty and for bailing me out when the dung hit the fan, and likewise my former shitmates **Benny Trickett**, 'Wild Cat' **Will Blanchard**, **Nigel Pollock** and **Nick van Gelder** for the 'education.'

Guy Gladstone and **Andrew Samuels** – true warriors. Respect.

And last but SO not least my accountant **Christine Anders** at Accurate Accounts. I mean, really – who thanks their *accountant* in a book? This has to be a WORLD EXCLUSIVE yeah? And I can't believe this but I'm actually *tearing up* as I write this 'cos if it wasn't for Christine I'd be on a bench by now, seriously, and there is NO way this book would have been written unless I'd done it with the stub of an old pencil on a discarded fish' n chip wrapper. I've sent so many of my clients to see Christine over the years and every one of them has returned and said – in hushed tones – "*she's... she's a fucking genius...*"

'Cos she is.

To all you **Bill Hicks** and **Hunter S. Thompsons** out there (you read the bit about projection right?) who keep fighting the

fight against the creatures of the commonplace, who speak

OUt against lies and oppression wherever you see it, even when you're frightened, *especially* when you're frightened, I salute you.

And thank

you for reading this book, big yourself up...

Or is it big up *yourself*?

That's the trouble with approaching fifty, hip enough to pick up on what's street, not hip enough to use it right.

Whatever...

I hope *Play From Your Fucking Heart* sowed some seeds and was a fun, easy read. As my grandfather said to me, not long before he died, "*as long as you've got a sense of humour– bugger everything else...*"

And that feels like a pretty good note to end on.

JH, London, November 2013

Soul Rocks is a fresh list that takes the search for soul and spirit mainstream. Chick-lit, young adult, cult, fashionable fiction & non-fiction with a fierce twist